— BARBARA BRACKMAN'S —
ENCYCLOPEDIA
of APPLIQUÉ

2000 Traditional and Modern Designs

◆

Updated History of Appliqué

◆

New! 5 Quilt Projects

C&T PUBLISHING

Text copyright © 2009 by Barbara Brackman

Artwork copyright © 2009 by C&T Publishing, Inc.

PUBLISHER: Amy Marson

CREATIVE DIRECTOR: Gailen Runge

ACQUISITIONS EDITOR: Susanne Woods

EDITOR: Deb Rowden

TECHNICAL EDITOR: Helen Frost and Sandy Peterson

COPYEDITOR/PROOFREADER: Wordfirm Inc.

COVER/BOOK DESIGNER: Kristy K. Zacharias

PRODUCTION COORDINATOR: Kirstie L. Pettersen

ILLUSTRATOR: Tim Manibusan

PHOTOGRAPHY BY Christina Carty-Francis and Diane Pedersen of C&T Publishing, Inc., unless otherwise noted.

Published by C&T Publishing, Inc., P.O. Box 1456, Lafayette, CA 94549

Library of Congress Cataloging-in-Publication Data

Brackman, Barbara.

[Encyclopedia of appliqué]

Barbara Brackman's encyclopedia of appliqué : 2000 traditional and modern designs, updated history of appliqué : new! 5 quilt projects / Barbara Brackman.

p. cm.

Includes bibliographical references and index.

Summary: "Features designs from the nineteenth and twentieth centuries arranged by design structure so that unknown patterns can be identified. Also included is a history of American appliqué"--Provided by publisher.

ISBN 978-1-57120-651-0 (paper trade : alk. paper)

1. Appliqué. I. Title. II. Title: Encyclopedia of appliqué.

TT779.B732 2009

746.44'5--dc22

2008045702

Printed in China

10 9 8 7 6 5 4 3 2 1

ACKNOWLEDGMENTS

I could not have done this book without the assistance of many friends and correspondents. First, I want to thank Cuesta Benberry and Joyce Gross for sharing their knowledge and their libraries. I am grateful also to other members of the American Quilt Study Group for their answers to my questions. And many thanks to researchers who indexed appliqué before I started to try to sort it all out—among them: Jeana Kimball and Elly Sienkiewicz for their work with nineteenth-century appliqué designs; Louise Townsend for her index to *Kansas City Star* patterns; Wilene Smith for answers about Nancy Page and other pattern sources; Merikay Waldvogel for her index to Anne Orr; Yvonne Khin and Judy Rehmel, whose books have served as my appliqué resources for years; Edna Van Das for her amazing index to the Nancy Cabot patterns; and Wilma Smith for her indexes to practically everyone, especially the prodigious Laura Wheeler.

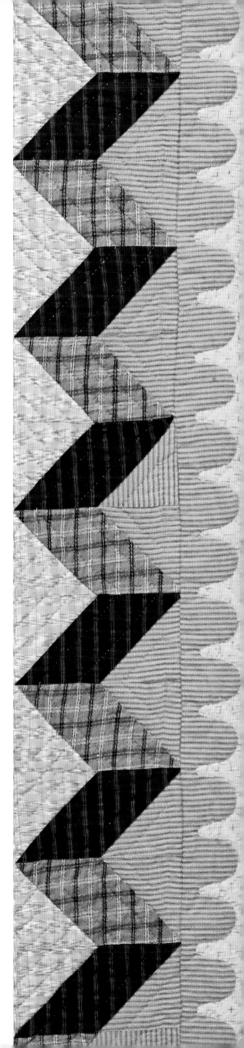

CONTENTS

ABOUT THE AUTHOR

Barbara Brackman became interested in quilt patterns as an undergraduate at the University of Kansas in the 1960s. At the back of the classroom in which she studied art history, she discovered drawers full of quilt blocks. These blocks were the collection of Carrie Hall, who had published a patchwork index in the 1930s entitled *The Romance of the Patchwork Quilt in America*. Determined to make a quilt in every design, Barbara started a file of quilt blocks. She soon realized, as Carrie Hall had, that one person could not hope to stitch a block in every pattern, much less a quilt. An index card on each, however, was possible, and over 25 years, Barbara's file grew to include thousands of quilt patterns.

In the 1980s, Barbara published the *Encyclopedia of Pieced Quilt Patterns* and, in 1993, the *Encyclopedia of Appliqué*. The latter has been out of print for several years. This new edition includes updated information about the pattern sources and current information about trends in appliqué history.

PREFACE

My first index of quilt designs, the *Encyclopedia of Pieced Quilt Patterns*, grew to eight volumes with 4,000 designs drawn from patterns published between 1835 and 1980. I long resisted indexing appliqué because the patterns seemed so diverse and unclassifiable. Appliqué did not appear to follow the geometric structures of pieced designs. In addition, the technique itself allowed much freedom to the individual quiltmaker, who could move leaves, stems, and flowers at will, creating designs quite different from the original model.

Appliqué designs imitate nature, with its seemingly infinite variety, and thus seem infinite themselves. But nature has been categorized into species and genera, so why shouldn't appliquéd designs fall into categories? Inspired by Linnaeus and other taxonomists, I began this index in the late 1980s and first published it in 1993.

The majority of the patterns indexed here were printed in books, periodicals, and catalogs published from 1835 through 1992. However, I did not include many designs that originated after 1960. And because the earlier commercial publications from before 1920 rarely included appliqué, some common patterns, as well as many uncommon ones, went unrecorded. Because a significant aspect of appliqué design would be missed if I referenced only published patterns, I also indexed designs that I found in antique quilts. I focused that research on appliquéd album or sampler quilts with dates actually inscribed on them; most unnamed patterns described as "from an album" will be followed by the date inscribed on the quilt.

The pictorial index enables you to find the name of an unknown pattern, but know that those names are highly arbitrary. Most are names used by people born after 1900. We know very little about what nineteenth-century quiltmakers called their quilts. At the turn of the twentieth century, when periodicals started recording names, the source was often an editor's or designer's whim.

I used to believe that every pattern had a name and that with persistence I could find it, but after spending years surrounded by drawings on index cards and tiny photocopied clippings, I learned to agree with quilt historian Florence Peto, who wrote in 1949, "It is not wise to be didactic about the nomenclature of quilt patterns." [1]

Chapter 1
THE HISTORY *of* APPLIQUÉ

"As American as Appliqué"

If the quilt is the quintessential American folk art, appliqué is the characteristic American quilt. Although needleworkers in many cultures have decorated cloth by applying layers of fabric, and some have combined the technique with quilting, the traditional red-and-green American quilt with its distinctive repeat of floral forms is unique. Like much else in our culture, the appliqué quilt is a recipe for the melting pot. Beginning with a stock of English bedding traditions, quilters added substantial parts of German design and contemporary decorative arts, spicing the mix with images from diverse immigrant and native folk arts.

Garden Wreath with Running Vine Border, estimated date 1840–1870. From the collection of Ruth Finley's family.

In her 1929 book *Old Patchwork Quilts and the Women Who Made Them*, Ruth Finley christened many traditional patterns. She described this quilt as an "elaborately conceived Garden Wreath quilt" with a border of an "exceptionally beautiful running vine." Wreaths with flowers at the four compass points are numbered 2.23 to 2.9 in the index.

Decorative appliqué traditions date back centuries. During the Renaissance in western Europe, the technique was used to ornament liturgical hangings and vestments, as well as secular clothing, bedding, and draperies. Never as common as woven pattern or added thread decoration, it was considered a type of embroidery, known as *intarsia* embroidery (German derived from an Italian word meaning "inlay" or "encrust"), which was most prevalent in Italy, Spain, and France.

Quilt historians Marie Webster and Schuppe Von Gwinner noted numerous examples of appliqué from the African continent. John Michael Vlach, an expert on African American arts, directed American eyes to the traditional appliqué hangings of several African regions and asked provocative questions about the transmission of design ideas. Most of the appliqué designs on bedcovers and hangings from Europe and Africa are pictorial narratives with religious, patriotic, or military themes, but among the pictures of warriors, royalty, animals, and mythical figures are floral and geometric designs much like American motifs. [2]

Left: An embroidered figure of a Mano chief, Liberia, Africa, before 1945. Right: A block from an appliquéd wallhanging of the Fon tribe, Benin, Africa, ca. 1900

Appliqué combined with quilting is less common in old-world cultures. Von Gwinner pinpointed the oldest surviving appliqué quilt as Swedish, attributed to 1303. She noted another Swedish quilt, made a century later, which anticipated many characteristics of American quilts. Appliquéd in repetitive blocks, it features stylized animals inside roundels (circles) from which four fleurs-de-lis sprout. [3]

Motifs drawn from a Swedish quilt, fifteenth century

Motifs drawn from an appliquéd quilt dated 1779, southeastern Germany—Although many of this quilt's motifs, such as the one on the bottom right, have little to do with American appliqué, the pot of flowers with the eight-lobed rosette bears evidence of German roots for American appliqué.

Several examples of appliquéd bedcovers and quilts survive from eighteenth-century Germany (not then a country but a group of independent states united by a common language). Like English and American quilts from the same period, German appliqué was often based on a medallion format with a central design focus—usually a large block surrounded by fields of patchwork.

THE RISE OF THE CONVENTIONAL APPLIQUÉ TECHNIQUE

Detail of a cutout chintz or Broderie Perse spread by an unknown maker, estimated date 1810–1850. From the collection of Mariana Aylward. Courtesy of the Kansas Quilt Project.

American seamstresses initially favored a type of appliqué called *Broderie Perse* (French for Persian embroidery), or cutout chintz, in which the decorative elements are cut from a print and stitched to a plain ground. The technique has been traced to seventeenth-century Europe, when the first printed chintzes became popular there. Numerous eighteenth-century examples survive in England, and it may be that the technique for making Broderie Perse quilts came to America with the English taste for chintzes. The style was popular enough in the early nineteenth century that English and American mills printed chintzes with figures designed to be cut and stitched onto quilt tops. [4]

Chintz appliqué quilts made in America between 1750 and 1840 shared several design conventions, including a medallion format framed with rows of borders. The designs had an oriental lushness, because the chintzes from which they were cut were heavily influenced by European interpretations of Asian art.

Major themes were the flowering tree (the tree of life) and a central vase holding many blooms, including true-to-life depictions of peonies, chrysanthemums, and roses next to fanciful representations of imaginary exotics. Color schemes were naturalistic greens, reds, browns, and yellows. Flowers were commonly cut from fabric with a white ground and rearranged on another white ground.

Broderie Perse, according to needlework historian Susan Burrows Swan, is a late nineteenth-century name for the older technique. In 1882, for example, English writers Sophia Caulfeild and Blanche Saward distinguished "true appliqué with plain colord [sic] stuffs" from Broderie Perse, or "appliqué with cretonne" (a synonym for chintz). To clarify the differences, I will call the latter cutout chintz and the former conventional appliqué, because so many patterns were called Conventional Rose or Conventional Tulip and because the technique is now the conventional method. [5]

Between 1775 and 1840, conventional appliqué was used in border designs of swags or leaves, primarily as accents to cutout chintz and piecing. Conventional appliqué blossomed in about 1840. The subordinate technique completely replaced cutout chintz within a few decades, so that after 1865, a cutout chintz quilt became a rarity. By the time Caulfeild and Saward described cretonne appliqué in 1882, it had almost disappeared in the United States, succeeded by a taste for the cleaner lines and formalized shapes of conventional appliqué.

Unknown woman in Peru, Illinois, about 1865—Appliquéd details were a popular feature of Civil War era clothing.

particularly for handscreens, where the flowers and leaves were formed of velvet and the stalks embroidered with gold bullion." A similar pamphlet, titled the *Lady's Guide to Embroidery and Appliqué*, said, "Appliqué is one of the most beautiful, and at the same time one of the easiest modes of embroidery and may be worked with great rapidity." These manuals, although "revised and enlarged" by American women, were probably direct copies of English material, as were most needlework publications of the period. Their meager patterns and material descriptions have more in common with intarsia embroidery than with American quilts, yet the sewing techniques are similar. [6]

If appliqué decorations were popular for clothing and household decorations, it would follow that girls learned the skill through patchwork. Textile historian Virginia Gunn noted commonalities in nineteenth-century quilts and clothing, hypothesizing that techniques such as the whipped seams found in template patchwork, corded binding, and the straight seams pressed to one side typical of piecework seams are components of quilts because quilts served as samplers for children's needlework training. Teachers might well have taught appliqué as it became an important decorative detail. [7]

After 1840, block patterns exploded in diverse, sophisticated design, with no gradual evolution from the simple to the complex. Most of the traditional patterns in this index can be traced to the first years of this style. Few of these patterns originated after 1865 and the end of the Civil War. It wasn't until twentieth-century pattern designers began reshaping appliqué that we saw another burst of innovative design.

The reasons for the genesis of conventional appliqué are many. They include changes in fashion, technology, and cultural adaptations. Georgiana Brown Harbeson, who wrote on American needlework, noted the fashion for appliquéd clothing in the 1840s and 1850s. She quoted the *Lady's Work Box Companion*: "Appliqué, combined with embroidery was much in vogue a few years since,

Fashion in home interiors of the middle and upper classes underwent a change in the first half of the nineteenth century. Jack Larkin, in *The Reshaping of Everyday Life 1790–1840*, discussed the absence of ornamental possessions in the average home early in the century. He quoted an 1828 letter from Margaret Hall who, awed by the luxuries in a South Carolina plantation, focused on "snow white quilts and draperies." By the 1840s, these items were far more common in the homes of a growing middle class. [8]

In the 1830s, a transformation occurred in the bedrooms of those wealthy enough to afford draperies. The typical American bed had been enclosed in hangings for privacy and warmth, but changes in fabrics and taste began to require open beds. Ideas about health affected style as people began to appreciate a fresh breeze. Bed hangings were thought to encourage miasmas (bad air that caused illness). Appliqué quilts and other striking bedding provided decorative emphasis on a bed without hangings.

Quiltmaking fashions that bloomed during the 1840s are entwined with the changes in appliqué. The block quilt replaced the medallion format as the major American style. Calicos and plain fabrics required for conventional appliqué were more suited to repetitive quilt blocks than was traditional chintz, with its limited number of repeats that could be cut. As the album or friendship quilt became a fad, the freedom of conventional appliqué meant that each donor to the group project could personalize her contribution.

Fashion is often dictated by changes in technology. In analyzing quiltmaking trends, one must always look to trends in fabric production. In the early nineteenth century, American mills, which were learning to compete with English and French cotton manufacturers, offered prints at prices that democratized fabric. Calico at 10 to 40 cents per yard meant that working families could afford cotton for a new dress or a quilt. New Hampshire school teacher Elizabeth Hodgdon, who earned $11 in 1832 for eleven weeks of teaching, was certainly cash poor by our standards, but her account book records that she purchased eight yards of calico at 14 cents per yard. The new, lower price of calicos democratized quiltmaking, enabling more American girls and women to take up the craft that had previously been the domain of the well-to-do. As cheaper calicos replaced more expensive chintzes, conventional appliqué replaced chintz appliqué. [9]

Fabric's lower price freed women from home textile production. No longer required to spin and weave, the average woman could devote her time to patchwork with purchased cotton. The mechanization of the pin-making industry probably affected the popularity of the appliqué technique, which requires much preparatory basting or pinning. Before 1840, most American pins were imported. The 1832 invention of an American pin machine meant a significant decrease in the price of a paper of pins, further democratizing certain needlework techniques.

Detail of an appliquéd quilt by Susan Mary Howarton (1831–1927), Indiana, estimated date 1850–1870. From the collection of Ollideen Wright. Courtesy of the Kansas Quilt Project.

Quilt historians Nancy Hornback and Ricky Clark pointed out the relationships between appliqué design and Germanic folk arts. Susan Mary Howarton's rather unusual design is a variation of the traditional German "sprouting heart." Although I did not index this design, it would be numbered 31—a bouquet with a central Rose of Sharon.

An important influence on the new look in appliqué quilts was the Pennsylvania Germans' adoption of the bedding of their neighbors of British ancestry. Pennsylvania Germans (often called the Pennsylvania Dutch) are descendants of immigrants from many of the German-speaking states who settled in southeastern Pennsylvania between 1683 and 1820. Primarily farmers and artisans, they were Protestants of the Lutheran and Reformed congregations. (Amish and other sectarians formed about 10 percent of their numbers.)

Slow to assimilate American culture, they continued to speak German, continued to work crafts such as furniture and metalwork in German style, and made their beds in German fashion, sleeping under heavy ticks more like feather beds than comforters. While their English American neighbors patched quilts and wove coverlets and blankets, generation after generation of Pennsylvania Germans persisted in filling homewoven ticks with straw and feathers.

Pennsylvania folklorist Jeannette Lasansky noted that Pennsylvania German dowry records, wills, and estates began listing quilts in about 1830, evidence of the period when they adopted the form of the three-layer bedcover fastened with a quilting stitch. Surviving quilts from midcentury Pennsylvania German families indicate that those families also adopted the standard English and American pieced patterns of stars, checks, and wheels. They did not, however, take up the Broderie Perse technique, instead preferring appliqué designs based on traditional German folk art motifs. They replaced the Chinese-inspired tree of life with three geometric flowers in a pot and the Persian chrysanthemum with an eight-lobed rosette, motifs that dominated American appliqué for the rest of the century. [10]

DESIGN SOURCES

Folk Dance Sampler, by Karla Menaugh, Barbara Brackman, and Jean Stanclift. Quilted by Rosie Mayhew. Lawrence, Kansas, 2002. 58″ × 58″.

In the early twenty-first century, we designed a series of reproduction appliqué patterns, using new color ideas and machine stitching techniques. Here we borrowed from Piece o' Cake designers Becky Goldsmith and Linda Jenkins, who popularized pieced backgrounds for appliqué. We also learned ideas from primitive/folk designer Jan Patek's simplified shapes and her updated muted red-and-green color schemes.

Our blocks, inspired by antique quilts, have formal symmetries. A line drawn down the center of the middle block shows that one side reflects the other in two-way mirror-image symmetry. The symmetry in the corner heart blocks is diagonal (ignore the asymmetrical birds). The center left block has four-way mirror-image symmetry, in which two lines following the seams or two diagonals create four identical quadrants.

Despite their diversity, appliqué patterns fall within certain structures, as folk arts usually do. Most nineteenth-century designs have a four-way mirror-image symmetry with four identical quadrants. Many designs feature a central motif with radiating units. Exceptions include blocks such as baskets, urns, and bouquets with two-way symmetry.

Most classic appliqué motifs indexed in this book—the standards that look so American to the quilt lover's eye—can be traced back centuries in European cultures. Carnations, peonies, pineapples, feathers, and flat rosettes are common in Jacobean embroidery, which is the English style that goes back

to the days of King James I in the seventeenth century. Other appliqué designs reflect nineteenth-century fashions in ornament. Grapes and grape leaves, eagles, wreaths, rising suns, and fleurs-de-lis decorated all manner of American objects.

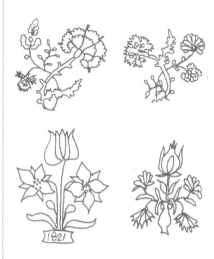

Top: Motifs drawn from an embroidered bedspread made in 1772 exemplify the English Jacobean traditions in needlework design.

Bottom: Motifs drawn from Pennsylvania German crafts—The design on the left is incised in a plate dated 1821; on the right is a design painted on a chest circa 1830.

Germanic tradition is apparent in the eight-lobed rosette and the three-lobed tulip—the two most popular elements in floral quilt patterns. Reinhard Peesch, a European folk art historian, described the rose that quilters call the Rose of Sharon as more a metaphor than a natural flower and noted its relationship to the eight-pointed star, often used in German folk arts and American quilts to represent a flower with stems and leaves. Simple rosettes with four, five, and six lobes are common in decorative arts ranging from Jacobean embroidery to the beadwork of the Great Lakes Indians through cowboy boots in the

1940s, but it is the eight-lobed rosette that dominates both German folk arts and nineteenth-century American appliqué. Had appliqué designs developed directly from English and French needlework traditions without Germanic influence, there would be far more emphasis on four- and five-lobed rosettes than we find in quilts made after 1840. Had needlework and ornament from the popular culture of that era affected quilt design, we would see far more emphasis on the realistic roses, pansies, and lilies found in the Berlin work (needlepoint) that was so fashionable during the golden age of appliqué. [11]

Rosettes and tulips are not the only design ideas shared by traditional German ornament and American appliqué. Peesch described potted flowers, usually featuring a "stem with three sprouting blooms," growing from a vessel with two slim handles. In addition to roses and tulips, the pots often sprout carnations with fanlike crowns, an image less common in American quilts than in German ornament or Jacobean embroidery. Peesch also described the pomegranate, a round fruit with many seeds visible through an oval incision. A similar motif is called the Love Apple in American quilt design. Other categories in Peesch's index of German folk design include the paired couple, the magic knot (an interlaced knot), the Basque cross (similar to a swastika), the heart, the eagle, and the Garden of Eden—all images repeated in many variations in American appliqué. A comparison of American appliqué designs to Germanic folk arts reveals numerous

similarities that are more than coincidence. It is likely that American appliqué developed when the Pennsylvania Germans adopted the bedding of the English Americans and translated the decorative motifs to their own design vocabulary. The Pennsylvania Germans, living in what cultural geographers identify as the central midlands, have had the same strong influence on the appliqué quilt that they had on other folkways, from coverlet weaving to barn architecture. [12]

Detail of an appliquéd wreath quilt inscribed "Fannie E. Cole 1858" in a corner block, Pennsylvania. Collection of Sandra Thlick and Katalin Stazer.

Fannie incorporated two classic floral images found across many cultures over many centuries. The "rose" viewed from above is a simple flattened shape. The "tulip" is portrayed in profile and often in triplicate. She used a reverse appliqué technique for the center of her roses, cutting a circle in the red-brown cotton to reveal the chrome orange fabric beneath.

Of course, some standard patterns in American quilt designs go beyond the conventionalized motifs of the Pennsylvania Germans. Between 1846 and 1852, the women of Baltimore and surrounding counties developed a style of appliqué that was quite luxuriant and naturalistic. Few of their elaborate patterns were repeated outside the area. Many seem to have been an individual whim or a brief fashion among a small group. Southern quiltmakers also developed distinctive appliqué designs not seen in the central midlands or the Midwest. Idiosyncratic designs have been traced from specific regions of the Carolinas, Kentucky, and Tennessee to the western states settled by Southerners. [13]

Two regional quilt patterns—Variations of the twin cornucopia and dove are from the Baltimore vicinity in the 1840s and 1850s. The medallion is from the Carolinas in the last half of the nineteenth century.

Detail of an appliquéd fruit and floral summer spread. Inscribed J. A. Caspar (?), Pennsylvania, estimated date 1840–1880.

This well-worn spread features the appliqué artist's favorite fabrics: Turkey red, green, and chrome orange on a white background. The red is sloughing off due to abrasion, a common problem with Turkey red. The green appears to be overdyed, first with Prussian blue and then with chrome yellow. Alkaline laundry soaps damage Prussian blue, so we can conclude that the splotches were probably caused by an unusually harsh washing. Techniques include reverse appliqué on the baskets and embroidery for the strawberry stems.

Appliqué's color scheme was as conventionalized as the patterns. The standard combination was red and green on white. Between 1840 and the Civil War, the red was usually a Turkey red calico, dyed in a lengthy process that produced an unusually fast and brilliant red dotted with paisley cones, florets, or geometrics of blue, green, yellow, black, or white. Plain red cottons became increasingly popular in the 1850s. By the last quarter of the century, reds for appliqué were nearly always plain fabrics.

The green cottons that formed the leaves were either printed or plain. Midcentury greens were overdyed—first colored blue and then yellow or vice versa. The two-step process eventually resulted in one or the other dye fading, leaving yellow-green or blue-green leaves. Popular accent shades were vivid double-pink prints, chrome yellow, and chrome orange (a shade of yellow-orange). The popularity of red and green on white seems likely to have been due to a combination of function and fashion. The choice of white for the large background areas was undoubtedly a practical matter. Undyed cotton was cheaper than calicos. Turkey red, although expensive, was unusually colorfast in an era of unstable dyes. The greens might fade but in an acceptable manner.

Color reflected the shades of nature, which had also been popular in naturalistic chintzes. Red and green was a traditional palette with Pennsylvania German folk artists working in other media, offering more evidence of their influence.

A second standard color scheme featured blue print calico on plain white background, probably influenced by bedding such as indigo blue and white woven coverlets. Classic blue-and-white quilts are nearly always done in a combination of indigo blues, or blue grounds printed with small white geometrics. Like Turkey red, colorfast indigo blue was more expensive but worth the price. [14]

Changes in Appliqué Style

The years 1840 to 1880 were the prime decades of the appliqué quilt, with those made in the first 25 years generally the finest. Post–Civil War quiltmakers were less inclined to add delicate details and fine quilting, especially stuffed work. Quilts made after 1865 tended to lack the elegance of prewar masterpieces.

Regional differences in style, as well as in pattern, developed throughout the decades. No other group can claim so distinctive a style as prewar Baltimore Album artists, but subtle preferences for pattern, contrast, and color combinations rose and fell. The postwar textile industry brought new Southern mills, which produced few calicos, the Northern mills' specialty. Postwar appliqué artists in the South were more likely to use plains over prints. At the risk of overgeneralizing about regional styles, I'll say that postwar Southerners who made appliqué quilts showed strong preferences for straight set blocks rather than diagonal sets, for rather wide sashing strips in contrasting shades, and for simple patterns, with tulips, either single or four set in a mirror-image repeat, being especially popular in some areas. During the last decades of that century, quilters in southeastern Pennsylvania, with its strong Pennsylvania German influence, developed a regional style based on color. They appliquéd designs to figured backgrounds, producing unusually colorful quilts by substituting bright blue or yellow prints for the traditional white neutral.

Pattern Sources

Appliqué pattern cut from a sewing machine catalog, ca. 1890, found in Lancaster County, Pennsylvania

A young needleworker intent upon her pattern, ca. 1900

"December 17, 1835. We attended the fair of St. Andrew's Church. The Council Chamber of the City Hall was tastefully decorated with evergreen, artificial flowers, etc. The variety of articles was much reduced, the prettiest having been disposed of. . . . I bought a . . . pattern card for patchwork." [15]

With rare exceptions, such as Phoebe George Bradford (1794–1840) of Wilmington, Delaware who wrote in her diary (left), nineteenth-century diarists and letter writers were silent about where they found their quilt patterns. One is tempted to believe that appliqué artists followed their own creative vision, but experience in classifying appliqué designs has taught me that one-of-a-kind appliqué quilts are rare. The many duplicates indicate that patterns were passed around in some fashion. Especially strong evidence of this are pairs or groups of quilts similar not only in pattern but also in sashing, border, and quilting.

Quilters obtained their patterns on paper—either bound into books and magazines or unbound "in the sheet." Early nineteenth-century pattern cards, like the one Phoebe bought at the church bazaar, have not survived, nor have any early patterns in the sheet. Bound patterns for quilts, pieced or appliqué, were rare until the 1890s. Those periodicals or needlework guides that did publish patterns often derived designs from England by plagiarizing British publications. Consequently, the few appliqué patterns published in the United States between 1840 and 1885 have little to do with American quilts. By the time published patterns were widely available, interest in appliqué had waned, so it wasn't until the revival of appliqué in the 1920s that there was an extensive body of appliqué designs in print.

Nineteenth-century quiltmakers were versed in many forms of needlework and probably used similar methods to obtain patterns for embroidery, quilting, and patchwork. Needleworkers have had pattern books available for centuries.

Davida Tenenbaum Deutsch, in an article entitled "Needlework Patterns and Their Use in America," listed books published in Germany, the Netherlands, Italy, France, and England during the early sixteenth century. Pennsylvania German embroiderers often copied their traditional designs from graphed patterns, which could easily be adapted to appliqué work. The German patterns probably reached an audience of quiltmakers beyond southeastern Pennsylvania, which is one way the German design influence may have diffused so thoroughly into American culture. [16]

Deutsch also noted the importance of sewing curricula published to teach poor girls needlework skills. Prominent were Lancasterian needlework instruction books, named for Joseph Lancaster (1778–1838), who developed the idea in England. The Baltimore school book, published in 1821, included illustrations and instructions for various designs. The book, published in Albany, New York, suggested that teachers create a pattern book "with handsome specimins [sic] for the imitation of scholars." One can imagine that needlework teachers taught appliqué using standard patterns in the same way they taught embroidery. Each teacher developing a curriculum for her school may have developed her own distinctive appliquéd designs or used versions published by others.

In the mid-nineteenth century, professional artists in many fields sold their own hand-drawn patterns to handcrafters who had less design skill. Phoebe Bradford's pattern card may have been hand drawn by a talented church member, as were those advertised in 1844 by the Ladies of the Episcopal Church in Weston, Connecticut, who held a fair to fund a new church. "Our Bedquilt patterns, such as French Cross, Feathered Star, Double Star, Double Chain, are beautiful." [17]

Such a scenario might explain similarities in the extraordinary Baltimore Album blocks. Some designs unique to the Baltimore quilts are related to theorem (stencil painting), a craft popular with women in the second quarter of the nineteenth century. Painting teachers designed and sold theorem stencils to their students. *Art Recreations*, published in 1860, instructed women in the techniques of making their own theorem stencils and advised them that the craft was "better adapted to fruits, birds and butterflies, than to landscapes and heads." Theorem conventions emphasized still-life designs with fruit-laden compotes and baskets full of flowers, many of which resemble the patterns numbered 42.6 in the index. [18]

Motifs drawn from a theorem painting (left) and an 1848 album quilt (right)

Few original theorem stencils survive, but it is obvious that they were in wide circulation during the years of the fad. Theorem painters cut stencils from what was called horn paper—a stiff, waterproof material made by coating pasteboard with linseed oil and turpentine. Cultured young women, trained to produce horn paper, stencils, and theorems, could easily transfer those skills to patchwork patterns. [19]

Craftsmen also used stencils to decorate furniture, tin ware, walls, and floors. Many of the designs popular with Pennsylvania German stencilers are similar to classic appliqué designs. It is easy to imagine how a quiltmaker might appropriate a stencil and pass it to her friends, spreading Pennsylvania German motifs into her community and beyond. There was also a minor tradition of stenciled quilts and spreads. Most that survive have been attributed to the years 1825–1835, indicating that the stenciled spread may be a forerunner of the conventional appliqué quilt, as transition from painted floral design to appliqué would be a simple process. [20]

Many appliqué artists probably transferred patterns directly from another quilt. Techniques for copying designs from textiles were common knowledge. In 1830, *Godey's Lady's Book* instructed seamstresses to take rubbings from needlework that they wanted to copy by fixing a sheet atop the piece and rubbing the surface with nutmeg, a technique that would work well with appliqué. *The Arts Companion*, published in 1749, described a tracing technique: "By the help of a Window, or a Glass held up to the Light, we copy all sorts of Prints, Designs and other pieces, upon Paper or Vellum, by fixing them to the paper or vellum we would draw upon. This is an easy and very good Contrivance for copying of the same size." Once she traced or rubbed a pattern onto paper, the seamstress could prick the lines with a pin. Placing the paper atop her fabric, she "pounced" the design by sprinkling a powder that sifted through the pinpricks onto the fabric. She could reuse the paper pattern for each block in her appliqué quilt and pass it on to admiring friends and relatives. [21]

Much evidence indicates that patterns were stored and circulated in the form of fabric blocks, which could also be traced or rubbed for duplication. Fabric patterns survive as single blocks or as parts of sampler quilts. The tradition of cloth patterns continued after the advent of pattern companies. The Ladies Art Company gave customers a choice of paper patterns or fabric blocks well into the twentieth century. [22]

Basted appliqué block, estimated date 1900–1940. This block makes me grateful for the freezer paper and wash-out glue available for appliqué preparation today. We may consider this to be an unfinished project, but it could have been saved as a pattern block for an unusual design. If I'd indexed it, I'd probably have included it next to 31.52 in the Bouquets/Central Rose of Sharon designs.

TERMINOLOGY

Pattern Names

Nineteenth-century women were far less descriptive about their quilts in diaries and letters than today's quilt historians would wish. I have read easily more than 100 such documents and found no descriptions of the appliqué technique, no terms for it, and precious few references descriptive enough to allow one even to guess what kind of quilt was in process. More helpful than most is Emily Hawley Gillespie's diary entry: "March 14, 1861. Piece on a quilt. Have 28 blocks done." [23]

Diarists, when they mentioned quilts at all, described them in terms of fabric or color, rarely technique or pattern. Typical is Elizabeth Porter Phelps: "April 19, 1767. Wednesday came here Miss Penn and Miss Polly to help me quilt a dark brown quilt." Seventy years later, Pamela Brown wrote, "April 12, 1837. Pieced a bed quilt of old calico." And Chastina Rix described her work: "September 22, 1849. Helped Sarah quilt, on her pink and white quilt like mine." [24]

The sparseness in descriptions indicates that names for specific patterns, whether pieced or appliquéd, were unimportant, if names were used at all.

There are intriguing exceptions, however. Elizabeth Myer wrote a letter in 1859 describing a "Flowering Almond" and left a quilt to her descendants much like the "Flowering Almond" numbered 16.65 in the index. In 1847, Parnel R. Grumly inscribed "The Peony and Prairie Flower No. 6″" on the back of her quilt, and in 1855, Jane Shelby wrote "Mississippi Beauty" on the back of hers. Elizabeth Range Miller left a "Rose of Sharon" in her 1857 will. [25]

Once we realize how little we know of nineteenth-century pattern names, the question of the "right" name for a pattern becomes moot. Arguments about the accuracy of "Princess Feather" versus "Prince's Feather" are absurd, because there are no correct names for traditional quilt patterns. Oral tradition changes, names fall out of use, regional and personal variations occur.

The task of indexing names for appliqué is easier than indexing pieced designs because fewer names for appliqué remain in print or in the oral tradition. Most pieced designs originated with commercial sources—the pattern companies and periodicals that generated patterns after 1890. But most standard appliqué designs developed decades before the advent of the commercial sources. By the time names were recorded in print, quiltmakers had lost interest in appliqué. The fact that fewer names for appliqué have been published is the major reason you will find many unnamed designs in this index. Today's nameless pattern may have had a mid-nineteenth century name that is now lost because it was never recorded, but my current belief is that the emphasis on pattern names developed after the heyday of the appliqué quilt.

Names for the Technique

Appliqué

The word *appliqué* is derived from a French verb *appliquér*, which has the same Latin root—*applicare* ("to attach to")—as our English *apply* ("to put on"). This standard name seems to have become common in the twentieth century, showing little use in the nineteenth. Although I have occasionally seen *pieced* in old diaries or letters, I have never seen *appliqué*. However, the term occasionally appeared in midcentury published sources. *The Lady's Work Box Companion* and *The Ladies Guide to Embroidery and Appliqué*, both published in Philadelphia in about 1850, contain the earliest American attributions I have yet seen. Because these are American revisions of English pamphlets, the name may have had little currency here.

In 1896, the *Ladies Home Journal* published an "appliqué daisy patch," but many writers seem to have had no term for the technique. In a scrapbook clipping from about 1890, the editor fumbled for words: "This style of patchwork is not so easily made as common patchwork." A 1911 *Ladies Home Journal* article on appliquéd pillow designs by Marie Webster had similar problems distinguishing between "the real patchwork method" and "pieced patchwork." The article did not use the word *appliqué*, but it does say that the seamstress "applied" the flowers. It may be that at the turn of the century, old words had passed out of the vernacular and the more formal or foreign word *appliqué* had not yet come into common use. [26]

Laidwork

The most commonly used old-fashioned synonym for appliqué was *laidwork*. Early twentieth-century authors often used both old and new terms to make it clear to their readers what they were talking about. During the 1920s, the Ladies Art Company used *appliqué* but explained that the technique once was called "laid work." *The American Woman* described "laidwork, that is the leaves, stems, 'rose,' etc. are cut from red and green cloth and felled to a square of white cotton." In her 1915 book, Webster used *appliqué* but also used "laid" or "laid-on work," among other terms. Nineteenth-century evidence of that term is sparse, but a South Carolina fair offered a prize for a "laid work quilt." [27]

Four-block appliqué quilt by Isabelle Wiswall Herman in Herman, New York, estimated date 1840–1880

The design combines inlaid and onlaid work in a pattern we call a Coxcomb Variation (number 19.75 in the index). The green corner units in each block were stitched onto the surface in laidwork or conventional appliqué. The red details were revealed in inlaid work, or what we call reverse appliqué. The borders were appliquéd in a technique we tend to call dogtooth appliqué.

Onlaid and Inlaid Work

Variations of the term *laidwork* were used to describe different types of appliqué. Caulfeild and Saward described "onlaid" and "inlaid" appliqué to discuss fabric added to a background versus the technique that cuts away background to reveal other layers. Today we call this last category "reverse appliqué" and associate it with Panama's San Blas Indians, who used it to create *mola* panels. Reverse appliqué was common in nineteenth-century American quilts, and many of the elements of the patterns indexed in this book could be created with onlaid or inlaid details. [28]

Needlework historian Susan Burrows Swan found a 1774 Savannah newspaper advertisement offering a reward for the return of a bed quilt with a tree of life design, "a large tree (inlaid work) with a peacock at the root and five small birds on the branches." The verbal distinction between inlay and onlay work continues in the cowboy bootmaking trade, in which most designs are cut out of the boot leg, revealing another color underneath (inlay). Bootmakers also add leather shapes on top (onlay). [29]

Patchwork

Other distinctions in turn-of-the-century quilt terminology include *patched* versus *pieced* for appliqué and piecework, respectively. In 1915, Webster used *patched quilt* as a synonym for *appliqué*. In the late 1920s, Ruby Short McKim told readers of her quilt pattern book: "There was a difference between the 'piece' quilts and 'patch' quilts. And contrary to what you might expect, the patch variety was the aristocrat and the pieced the poor relation. For 'patch,' sometimes called 'sewed-on' or 'laid work' meant the appliqués and required new cloth." [30]

In the 1930s, writers describing quilts consistently use the word *appliqué* as the standard term. By that point, they no longer needed to explain that *appliqué* was a synonym for anything. Today's quilters would be confused by patterns for laidwork, sewed-on, or felled quilts, though these old-fashioned terms linger in the vernacular. In 1991, I interviewed Texan Arthur Lambrecht, who'd been making quilts since 1910. He described his quilts as "laid work or appliqué." [31]

Detail of appliquéd block, estimated date 1880–1910. The seamstress combined old-fashioned appliqué with new fashions in embroidery to stitch this block, a variation of what I've labeled Four Fleur-de-lis and numbered as 6. Plain Turkey red is a difficult fabric to date because quilters used it from the 1840s into the 1940s. The best clue here is the embroidery stitch outlining the appliqué: the briar stitch was popular in crazy quilts and other embroidery projects after 1880.

THE DECLINE OF APPLIQUÉ

Appliqué quilts fell out of favor toward the end of the nineteenth century. Again, changes in fashion, technology, and American culture affected the technique's popularity. New quilt styles developed when the passion for Turkey red prints was replaced by crazes for brown calicos, complex shirting prints, and newly inexpensive silks. Brown cotton log cabin quilts were a fad in the 1870s, followed by silk crazy quilts in the 1880s.

As aniline dyes created in laboratories began to dominate the market after 1870, cottons became less reliable. Green was especially fugitive, prone to fade to shades of brown—the reason so many red, tan, and white appliqué quilts survive. After 1900, women may have abandoned appliqué because they could not find fast fabrics in appropriate shades. Former mill worker Harriet Robinson complained in 1898, "As for cheap American prints, who prefers to buy them nowadays? Certainly no woman who remembers with affection the good, pretty, durable and washable . . . old time calico." [32]

During those decades, sewing machines became commonplace in American homes, having a significant impact on the handwork that appliqué required. Girls who received needlework education after the machine's advent lacked hand-sewing skills and the incentive to practice them. Many appliqué quilts made in the last quarter of the nineteenth century reflect these lower standards. Curves lack grace, patterns lack detail, and stitches lack fine technique. Some women used their new machines to fasten their appliqué work, but only a few could achieve the complexity of hand appliqué with the machine stitch.

Just as interest in appliqué waned, printed patterns began to replace design passed hand to hand. National magazines and periodicals created national styles emphasizing new and complex pieced patterns. The Ladies Art Company, one of the first to publish patchwork patterns in the sheet, showed only 19 appliquéd designs out of 400 patterns in their turn-of-the-century catalog *Diagrams of Quilts, Sofa and Pin Cushion Patterns*. Taste and technology combined to make appliqué an old-fashioned and nearly forgotten art in most of the country. One exception was southeastern Pennsylvania, where women continued making appliqué quilts through the first decades of the new century.

THE APPLIQUÉ REVIVAL

Rose appliqué by Anna Todd McCann (1839–1963), Kansas, 1942. Collection of Maine Todd. Courtesy of the Kansas Quilt Project.

Anna McCann likely used a kit or a pattern for the quilt she made during World War II, waiting for news of her soldier husband. Even without the family story, we would date this quilt to the 1930–1950 era because of design and techniques. The set is based on a medallion rather than the block; the roses have five lobes rather than the more symmetrical six or eight. The technique combines appliqué and embroidery, and the color scheme is a softer pink and green rather than the old-fashioned bright red and green.

Two flappers with bobbed hair, short skirts, and cloche hats, ca. 1925

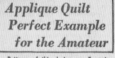

Applique Quilt Perfect Example for the Amateur

Patterns of this design are 5 cents, stamps or coin. Address Nancy Cabot, Chicago Tribune, or call at one of the Tribune Public Service offices: One South Dearborn street or Tribune Tower.

Kentucky Columbine.

BY NANCY CABOT.

For the beginning quilt maker who is thinking of making an attempt at applique work, "Kentucky Columbine" is one of the many fascinating blocks which should be given consideration. Set together on a pale yellow background, woodland violet and green are the predominant colors. To these are added a dash of orange which is most effective and which carries out the old two-and-one color rule. Sixteen applique blocks are set together with nineteen plain ones in an arrangement suggested on the pattern.

A Nancy Cabot column from the *Chicago Tribune* in the 1930s shows a typical commercial format. Readers could buy the full-size pattern for a nickel. Nancy advised pale yellow, violet, and green for the Kentucky Columbine with "a dash of orange."

Iris by Hannah Haynes Headlee (1866–1943), Kansas, estimated date 1935–1940. Collection of the Kansas Museum of History.

A mid-twentieth-century appliqué made without benefit of commercial pattern is a rarity. Hannah Headlee designed her own quilts and dyed her own fabrics to obtain the range of color she wanted in this masterpiece quilt. She was a watercolor artist and a china painter, a talented woman who finished seven marvelous quilts in her 60s and 70s.

In 1917, *Hearth and Home* magazine announced "the old-time 'laid-work' or appliqué patchwork has come in again." After decades of neglect, the quiltmaking public showed a renewed fascination with the technique. Taste, however, relegated the classic red and green floral quilts to the attic. Homemakers responded to a different look characterized by new fabrics, patterns, and color schemes. Marie Webster, designing for the *Ladies Home Journal*, was a major factor in the change. She first called for a new look in a 1911 article "The New Patchwork Quilts." Her innovations included naturalistic florals, a contrast to the abstracted roses and tulips of the nineteenth century. She harmonized light colors to match twentieth-century interior design and based many of her patterns on the medallion format rather than the block repeat. She presented her original designs by taking advantage of technological and style changes in magazine illustrations. Colored pictures specified the desired shades, and new page designs pictured the whole quilt as a rectangular composition, minimizing the earlier emphasis on a single block and maximizing the importance of border and edge. [33]

During the 1920s, appliqué multiplied in published sources. The 1922 version of the Ladies Art catalog had a new name, *Quilt Patterns: Pieced and Appliquéd*, and a new section on "attractive appliqué designs with borders." Several cottage industries, like that of Carlie Sexton, who wrote for *Better Homes and Gardens*, sold patterns closely copied from antique quilts. A few companies followed Marie Webster's lead with modern designs. Two of the most innovative were *Modern Priscilla* and *Needlecraft Magazine*.

As the 1920s ended, more designers responded to the modern look. One widely syndicated artist was Florence LaGanke Harris, who wrote a column under the name Nancy Page. Although her pieced patterns were traditional, her appliquéd designs were modern versions of the old appliqué sampler and were presented as series designs based on themes such as children's toys or the zodiac. (See Series patterns numbered in the 70s.)

Loretta Leitner Rising wrote a daily column for the *Chicago Tribune* from 1933 through the 1940s under the name Nancy Cabot. She revived traditional appliqué patterns but also invented numerous designs in the 2,000

patterns she published, which also appeared under different pen names in the *Progressive Farmer*, the *New York Daily News*, and other periodicals. Nancy Cabot patterns are the largest source of twentieth-century appliqué (note how many designs she originated in the patterns numbered 34 and 35). Despite her amazing production, she was less influential than less prolific designers like Webster and Page. Far more quilts survive in their designs than in Cabot's quirky blocks.

In the index, I marked patterns I believe to have been designed by twentieth-century artists with a "D." Traditional nineteenth-century designs are marked with a "T." My list of criteria for categorizing a pattern as "D" is short and rather subjective. The first is that I have not seen any evidence of the design in nineteenth-century quilts. The second is merely that it *looks like* a twentieth-century design. New color schemes made possible by improved aniline dyes are notable on the quilts if not the patterns. Pinks, lavenders, and shades of tangerine replaced the Turkey red cottons and indigo blues. Distinctive light greens with a bluish-gray cast replaced the dark greens so prone to fading.

Although most patterns were printed in black and white, the designers often suggested color. Nancy Cabot communicated the fashionable look effectively in her 1933 description of an 1840 pattern. "In the early days of its history only strong colors were available, and, like other old patterns of its time, it was executed in bright reds and greens. A twentieth-century quiltmaker would undoubtedly prefer dainty pastel shades." Marie Webster included actual fabric swatches in her mail-order patterns to assist the customer with color selection. [34]

The change in color schemes related to home-decorating trends. For years, the kitchens, bathrooms, and bedding of the well-to-do had been white, the color of cleanliness. But modern decorating dictated color-coordinated pastel kitchens and bathrooms, a compromise between color and hospital standards for sanitation because pale colors showed the dirt as well as white did. When white was the fashion, magazines recommended white bedspreads rather than "unsightly" and "unhealthy" patched quilts, but as light colors became fashionable, light-colored quilts became the bedding recommended by the home improvement experts. [35]

Modern quilts were more than a new color scheme, however. Symmetries moved away from formal, four-way mirror-image blocks or the bouquet of three tulips. Flowers undulated across the block, echoing art nouveau naturalism. Blocks often featured a single flower rather than a symmetrical bouquet. Medallion arrangements were constructed with concentric borders of graceful florals.

The eight-lobed rosette no longer dominated, although florals remained the primary subject matter. A wider variety of species was depicted; pansies, poppies, and irises were especially popular. Roses remained important, but like other flowers, they were appliquéd with naturalistic shape and shading. Many of the abstracted florals had four, five, or six petals—motifs that had been popular in European embroidery and other decorative arts for centuries but that had played a minor part in American appliqué between 1840 and 1920. Pictorial designs went beyond florals. Sunbonnet Sue and her grown-up counterpart, the Colonial Lady, were fashionable, as were butterflies, cuddly animals, and nursery rhyme characters.

Although new appliqué designs were numerous in publications after 1915, pieced patterns continued to dominate the commercial pattern network. The syndicated column that appeared under the names Laura Wheeler and Alice Brooks, for example, included four appliqué designs among 90 patterns in their newspaper ads of the 1930s. Ruby McKim's *101 Quilt Patterns*, published in 1931, contained only 11 patterns with appliqué work. A few companies, like Boag, Rainbow, and Webster's Practical Patchwork, specialized in appliqué or embroidery over pieced patterns, and appliqué was the mainstay of the quilt kit industry, a facet of the pattern business that expanded from 1920 to 1960. Paragon, Rainbow, and Bucilla each sold their own versions of elaborate floral medallion kits. During the 1950s and 1960s, as interest in quiltmaking faded and patterns disappeared from periodicals, quilters who did any appliqué work relied on kits. [36]

From 1950 to 1970, few designers generated new patterns of any kind; one exception was the Laura Wheeler/Alice Brooks syndicate. Their artists continued to produce simple patterns for kittens, puppies, flowers, and cowboys through quiltmaking's lean years.

Floral Bouquet, by Shirley and Shirlene Wedd. Kansas, 1997. 86″ × 92″.

Mother-daughter team Shirley and Shirlene Wedd designed a medallion featuring Kansas botanicals for the Kaw Valley Quilters Guild using ideas and techniques developed in classes by Elly Sienkiewicz. The quilt (the photo shows the quilt top before quilting) was exhibited in the 1998 Baltimore Album Revival Quilt Show and Contest. Shirley's design for the central vase with thistles, sunflowers, and trumpet flowers is based on traditional patterns numbered as 42 in the index.

Although piecework was the early focus of the 1970s quilt revival, innovative appliqué designs by women such as Jean Ray Laury, Virginia Avery, and Chris Wolf Edmonds influenced many others to create original pattern and pictorial appliqué.

In the late 1980s, a flurry of interest in collecting Baltimore Album quilts inspired seamstresses to look back to the mid-nineteenth century for inspiration. Elly Sienkiewicz's series of Baltimore Album pattern books and Jeanna Kimball's designs for traditional appliqué gave quiltmakers new access to complex blocks. [37]

In the first edition of this book, published in 1993, I wrote, "As appliqué again comes into its own, we will see quiltmakers at the turn of the twenty-first century creating quilts to equal the masterpieces of the 1840s and 1930s." Fifteen years later, I am pleased to note, "I told you so!" The 1990s saw an explosion of new ideas, new techniques, and stunning reproductions, a trend that continues into the new century. This is indeed the golden age of appliqué.

Footnotes

1. Florence Peto, *American Quilts and Coverlets* (New York: Chanticleer Press, 1949), 21.

2. Marie Webster, *Quilts: Their Story and How to Make Them* (New York: Doubleday, Page and Co., 1915); Schuppe Von Gwinner, *The History of the Patchwork Quilt* (West Chester, PA: Schiffer, 1988); John Michael Vlach, *The AfroAmerican Tradition in the Decorative Arts* (Cleveland, OH: The Cleveland Museum of Art, 1978), 44–54.

3. Von Gwinner, 57–63.

4. Jinny Beyer, *The Art and Technique of Creating Medallion Quilts* (McLean, VA: EPM, 1982).

5. Susan Burrows Swan, *Plain and Fancy: American Women and Their Needlework, 1700–1850* (New York: Holt, Rinehart and Winston, 1977); Sophia Frances Anne Caulfeild and Blanche C. Saward, *The Dictionary of Needlework* (London: L. Upton Gill, 1882), 10.

6. Georgiana Brown Harbeson, *American Needlework* (New York: Bonanza Books, 1938), 136; *The Lady's Work Box Companion* (Philadelphia: J. & J. L. Gihon, undated), 26; *The Lady's Guide to Embroidery and Appliqué* (Philadelphia: W. A. Leary, ca. 1850).

7. Virginia Gunn, "Template Quilt Construction and Its Offshoots: From Godey's Lady's Book to Mountain Mist," in Jeannette Lasansky (ed.), *Pieced by Mother: Symposium Papers* (Lewisburg, PA: Oral Traditions Project: 1988), 69–72.

8. Jack Larkin, *The Reshaping of Everyday Life 1790–1840* (New York: Harper and Row, 1988), 146.

9. Letter from Elizabeth Hodgdon, quoted in Thomas Dublin, *Farm to Factory: Women's Letters 1830–1860* (New York: Columbia University Press, 1981), 56.

10. Jeannette Lasansky, *A Good Start: The Aussteier or Dowry* (Lewisburg, PA: Oral Traditions Project, 1990), 43.

11. Reinhard Peesch, *The Ornament in European Folk Art*, transl. Ruth Michaelis-Jena and Patrick Murray (New York: Alpine Fine Arts Collection, 1982).

12. I am grateful to Nancy Hornback for calling my attention to Peesch's work and the similarities between American quilt design and German folk art. Nancy Hornback, *Quilts in Red and Green: The Flowering of Folk Design in 19th Century America* (Wichita, KS: Wichita-Sedgwick County Historical Museum, 1992).

13. Wilbur Zelinsky, *The Cultural Geography of the United States* (Englewood Cliffs, NJ: Prentice Hall, 1973).

14. Hornback, 3.

15. Phoebe George Bradford, "The Diaries of Phoebe George Bradford," in Wilson W. Emerson (ed.), *Delaware History* (1974), Wilmington, DE.

16. Davida Tenenbaum Deutsch, "Needlework Patterns and Their Use in America," *The Magazine Antiques*, vol. CXXXIX, no. 2, 368–381 (February 1991); Philadelphia Museum of Art, *Pennsylvania German Art 1683–1850* (Chicago: University of Chicago Press, 1984), 307.

17. Deutsch. Bridgeport, CT, *Republican Farmer*, vol. XXXV, no. 1792, 3 (August 20, 1844).

18. Levina B. Urbino and Henry Day, *Art Recreations* (Boston: J. E. Tilton, 1860), 145.

19. Vicki Mcintyre. "Theorem Paintings," *Early American Life*, August 1981, 28.

20. Diana Church, "The Baylis Stenciled Quilt," in *Uncoverings 1983* (Mill Valley, CA: American Quilt Study Group, 1984), 75.

21. *Godey's Lady's Book*, January 1830, 13, quoted in Margaret Vincent, *The Ladies Work Table: Domestic Needlework in Nineteenth Century America* (Allentown, PA: Allentown Art Museum, 1988); *The Arts Companion, or a New Assistant for the Ingenious in Three Parts* (London and Dublin, 1749), quoted in Deutsch, 376.

22. Wilene Smith, "Quilt Blocks—Or—Quilt Patterns," *Uncoverings 1986* (Mill Valley, CA: American Quilt Study Group, 1987).

23. Emily Hawley Gillespie, *A Secret to Be Burried* [sic]: *The Diary of Emily Hawley Gillespie, 1858–1888*, Judy Nolte Lensink (ed.) (Iowa City: University of Iowa Press, 1989), 43.

24. Diaries of Elizabeth Porter Phelps, Pamela Brown, and Chastina Rix, quoted in Lynn Bonfield, "Diaries of New England Quilters Before 1860," *Uncoverings 1989*, vol. 9 (San Francisco: American Quilt Study Group, 1989), 189, 192.

25. Letter from Elizabeth Nessly Myer, March, 24, 1860, quoted in Kay Atwood, *Mill Creek Journal* (Ashland, OR: Author, 1987), 120; Quilt #10.398, Shelburne Museum, Shelburne, VT; Karoline Patterson Bresenhan and Nancy O'Bryant Puentes, *Lone Stars: A Legacy of Texas Quilts, 1836–1936* (Austin: University of Texas Press, 1986), 40; Bets Ramsey and Merikay Waldvogel, *The Quilts of Tennessee: Images of Domestic Life Prior to 1930* (Nashville, TN: Rutledge Hill, 1986), 9.

26. Jane Benson, "Designs for Patchwork Quilts," *Ladies Home Journal*, November 1896, 24; Marie Webster, "The New Patchwork Quilts," *Ladies Home Journal*, January 1911.

27. *Catalog of Quilts and Quilting* (St. Louis: Ladies Art Company, undated), 1; *The American Woman*, undated clipping; Webster, *Quilts*; Virginia Gunn, "Quilts at Ohio Fairs," *Uncoverings 1989*, vol. 9 (San Francisco: American Quilt Study Group, 1989), 126.

28. Caulfeild and Saward, 8.

29. Swan, 228.

30. Marie Webster, *Quilts: Their Story and How to Make Them*, 94. Ruby Short McKim, *101 Quilt Patterns*, (Independence, MO: McKim Studios, 1931), 16.

31. Telephone interview with Arthur Lambrecht, November 18, 1991.

32. Harriet H. Robinson, *Loom and Spindle or Life Among the Early Mill Girls* (New York: Thos. Y. Crowell, 1898), 212.

33. Marie Webster, "The New Patchwork Quilts." *Ladies Home Journal*.

34. Nancy Cabot, "Rose of 1840," *Chicago Tribune*, July 16, 1933.

35. Harvey Green, *The Uncertainty of Everyday Life 1915–1945* (New York: Harper Collins, 1992), 184–185. "Bed-Clothes," *Arthur's Home Magazine*, October 1883, 63. For more on the changes influenced by modernism, see my book *Making History: Quilts & Fabric from 1890–1970* (Lafayette, CA: C&T Publishing, 2007).

36. Merikay Waldvogel, "Anne Orr's Quilts," *Uncoverings 1991*, vol. 11 (San Francisco: American Quilt Study Group, 1991), 21.

37. Elly Sienkiewicz's books include *Spoken Without a Word* (Washington, DC: Author, 1983) and *Baltimore Beauties and Beyond*, vol. 1 and 2 (Lafayette, CA: C&T Publishing). Jeanna Kimball's books include *Reflections of Baltimore* and *Red and Green: An Appliqué Tradition* (Bothell, WA: That Patchwork Place, 1989 & 1990).

FOUNDATION ROSE & PINE TREE

Foundation Rose & Pine Tree, by Georgann Eglinski, Lawrence, Kansas. Machine quilted by Lori Kukuk, 2008. 42″ × 42″.

The name for the block numbered 13.13 in the index is Foundation Rose and Pine Tree, which comes from a 1957 Shelburne Museum catalog. We can see a Foundation Rose in the basic center floral, but the corner vegetation looks far more like fruit than pine trees. Today's quilters might call these cherries, as Jeana Kimball did in her 1989 book.

Georgann Eglinski based her reproduction quilt on 7½″ × 7½″ squares so she'd have take-along handwork, but you could also appliqué this as four 15″ × 15″ blocks. The original had a plain border, a perfect spot to show off fancy quilting by hand or machine.

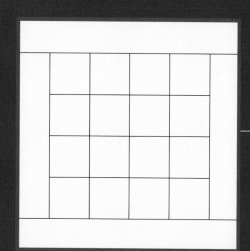

QUILT SIZE: 42″ × 42″

BLOCK SIZE: 7½″ × 7½″

BORDER WIDTH: 6″

YOU NEED:

16 appliquéd blocks

Plain border

FABRIC REQUIREMENTS

Ivory plain or low-contrast print for block background, border, and binding: 2¾ yards

Red plain or monochromatic print for appliqué pieces: ½ yard

Green plain or monochromatic print for appliqué pieces: ¾ yard

Golden yellow plain or monochromatic print for appliqué pieces: ¼ yard

Backing: 2⅝ yards

Batting: 46″ × 46″

CUTTING INSTRUCTIONS

Cut the appliqué pieces using the patterns on page 29. For hand appliqué, add a scant ¼″ seam allowance.

From ivory

Cut 16 squares 9″ × 9″ for block backgrounds. Trim to 8″ × 8″ after the appliqué is complete.

Cut 2 lengthwise strips 6½″ × 30½″ for side borders.

Cut 2 lengthwise strips 6½″ × 42½″ for top and bottom borders.

Cut 5 strips 2¼″ × width of fabric for binding.

From red

Piece A: Cut 80.

Piece C: Cut 4.

From green

Piece A: Cut 112.

Piece B: Cut 16.

From golden yellow

Piece A: Cut 32.

SEWING INSTRUCTIONS

Appliquéing the blocks

Press each background piece into quarters diagonally so you have lines for placement.

Placement lines

Prepare the appliqué pieces using your favorite method.

Arrange the pieces and baste, pin, or glue them in place.

Stitch the pieces using your favorite technique. Trim the blocks to 8″ × 8″.

Sew 4 blocks together to make larger blocks. Repeat to make a total of 4 large blocks.

Place and stitch piece C over the seamlines as shown.

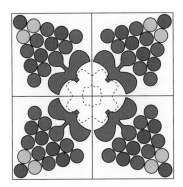

Placement for piece C

SETTING THE QUILT

Make 2 rows of 2 large blocks each. Join the rows. Press.

Add the side borders. Press.

Add the top and bottom borders. Press.

QUILTING

Lori Kukuk machine quilted a flamboyant feather in the border and more feathers in the white spaces between the blocks. She echoed the appliqué patches by stitching 1/16″ around them to add dimension.

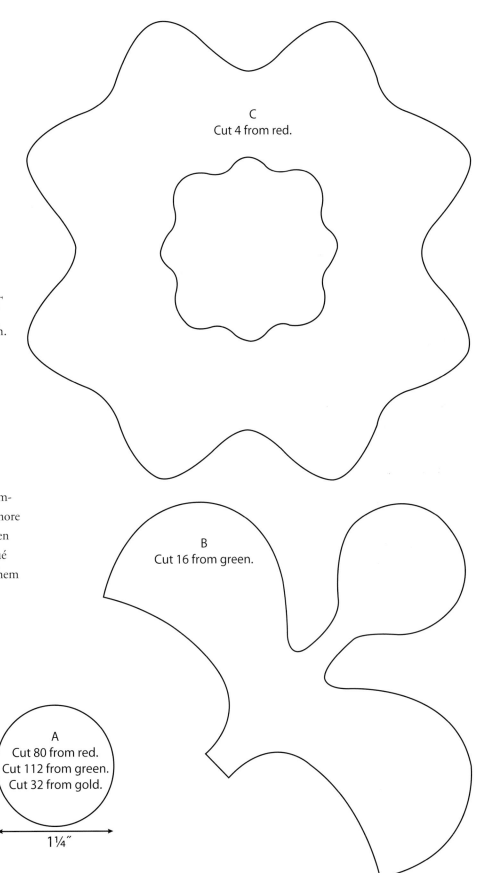

C
Cut 4 from red.

B
Cut 16 from green.

A
Cut 80 from red.
Cut 112 from green.
Cut 32 from gold.

1¼″

OAK LEAF & ORANGE PEEL

(Oak Leaf and Orange Peel) Bowden Family Quilt, by Bobbi Finley, Williamsburg, Virginia, 2003–2005. 79″ × 95″.

Bobbi Finley began this quilt in 2003 to take her mind off incoming Hurricane Isabel. While leafing through a catalog from the Shelburne Museum, she found a design called Oak Leaf and Orange Slice. The pattern is similar to the Four Plus Four Elements—Reels category on page 85 in the index of this book.

Bobbi dedicated the quilt, which took two and a half pleasant years of handwork, to her mother's ancestors, the Bowden family, who had settled in Mandarin, Florida, in the 1780s. The oak leaves symbolize the region's live oak

trees hung with Spanish moss. The orange peel or orange slice reminds her of Mandarin, named for the oranges grown there. Bobbi's family was among those who grew mandarins. She chose indigo blue to recall her ancestors who came as indentured servants more than 200 years ago from the Mediterranean to work in the indigo fields at New Smyrna, Florida.

Bobbi's quilt, although only two colors, is quite scrappy. The fabric requirements listed here will give you some variety, but you may want to buy more blues and tans for a scrappier look.

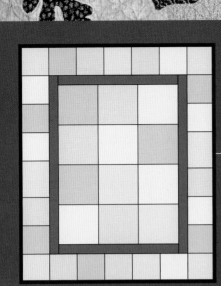

QUILT SIZE: 79" × 95"

BLOCK SIZE: 16" × 16"

BORDER WIDTHS: 3½", 12"

YOU NEED:

12 appliquéd blocks

Appliquéd inner border

Appliquéd outer border

FABRIC REQUIREMENTS

6 different tan and pale brown prints for block backgrounds, outer border, and appliqué pieces: 1¼ yards each

Small blue print for inner border and appliqué pieces: 1½ yards

Large blue print for inner border and appliqué pieces: 2⅛ yards

Indigo blue print for appliqué pieces and binding: 2¾ yards

3 different blue prints for appliqué pieces: ¾ yard each

Backing: 7 yards (pieced widthwise)

Batting: 83" × 99"

CUTTING INSTRUCTIONS

Cut the appliqué pieces using the patterns on pages 33–34. For hand appliqué, add a scant ¼" seam allowance.

From tan and light brown prints

Cut a total of 12 squares 17½" × 17½" for block backgrounds. Trim to 16½" × 16½" after the appliqué is complete.

Cut a total of 10 rectangles 12½" × 12" and 2 rectangles 12½" × 14" for side outer borders.

Cut a total of 10 rectangles 12½" × 11½" for top and bottom outer borders.

Cut a total of 4 squares 12½" × 12½" for outer border corners.

Piece E: Cut a total of 76 for inner borders.

From small blue print

Cut 2 lengthwise strips 4" × 48½" for top and bottom inner borders. Set aside leftover fabric for appliqué pieces.

From large blue print

Cut 2 lengthwise strips 4" × 71½" for side inner borders. Set aside leftover fabric for appliqué pieces.

From indigo blue print

Cut 2 lengthwise strips 1¾" × 79½" for appliquéd scallop for top and bottom outer borders.

Cut 2 lengthwise strips 1¾" × 95½" for appliquéd scallop for side outer borders.

Using pattern F, mark and cut scallops along one edge of above 4 strips.

Cut 4 strips 2¼" × length of fabric for binding.

Set aside leftover fabric for appliqué pieces.

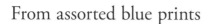

From assorted blue prints

Piece A: Cut a total of 12 for blocks.

Piece B: Cut a total of 48 for blocks.

Piece C: Cut a total of 48 for blocks; cut a total of 34 for outer borders.

Piece D: Cut a total of 48 for blocks.

SEWING INSTRUCTIONS

Appliquéing the blocks

Press the block background pieces into quarters diagonally, vertically, and horizontally, creating lines for placement.

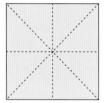

Placement lines

Prepare the appliqué pieces using your favorite method.

Arrange the pieces and baste, pin, or glue them in place.

Stitch the pieces using your favorite technique. Trim the blocks to 16½" × 16½".

Appliquéing the inner border

Prepare the appliqué pieces using your favorite method.

Arrange the pieces and baste, pin, or glue them in place. Position 16 pieces on each of the top and bottom borders and 20 pieces on each of the side borders.

**Note:** The appliqué pieces at the ends of the side borders will be added after the borders are sewn to the quilt.

Stitch using your favorite technique.

Piecing and appliquéing the outer border

Stitch together 5 rectangles 12½" × 12" and 1 rectangle 12½" × 14" to make each side border background. Press.

Stitch together 5 rectangles 12½" × 11½" to make each top and bottom border background. Add a square 12½" × 12½" to each end. Press.

Prepare the appliqué pieces using your favorite method.

Arrange the pieces and baste, pin, or glue them in place.

**Note:** The appliqué pieces over the border corner seams will be added after the borders are sewn to the quilt.

Leaves over seams

Stitch using your favorite technique.

Baste the blue scalloped pieces to the outside edges of the borders by stitching a basting line (hand or machine) ⅛" inch from the straight edge.

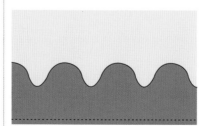

Baste straight edge.

Stitch the curved edges using your favorite technique.

Leave the ends of the pieces free until you have set the outer border together.

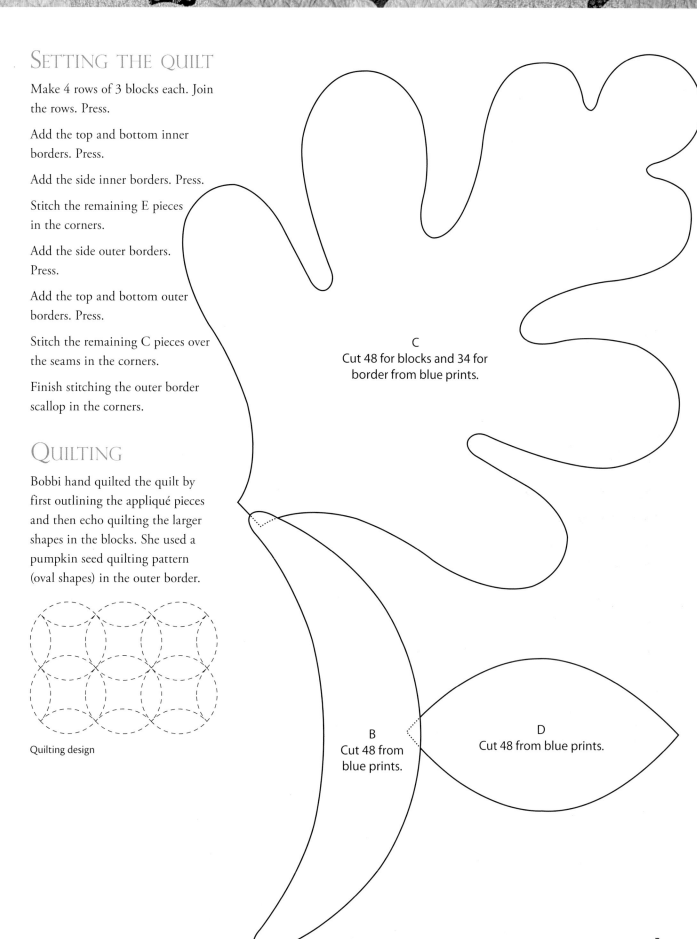

SETTING THE QUILT

Make 4 rows of 3 blocks each. Join the rows. Press.

Add the top and bottom inner borders. Press.

Add the side inner borders. Press.

Stitch the remaining E pieces in the corners.

Add the side outer borders. Press.

Add the top and bottom outer borders. Press.

Stitch the remaining C pieces over the seams in the corners.

Finish stitching the outer border scallop in the corners.

QUILTING

Bobbi hand quilted the quilt by first outlining the appliqué pieces and then echo quilting the larger shapes in the blocks. She used a pumpkin seed quilting pattern (oval shapes) in the outer border.

Quilting design

C
Cut 48 for blocks and 34 for border from blue prints.

B
Cut 48 from blue prints.

D
Cut 48 from blue prints.

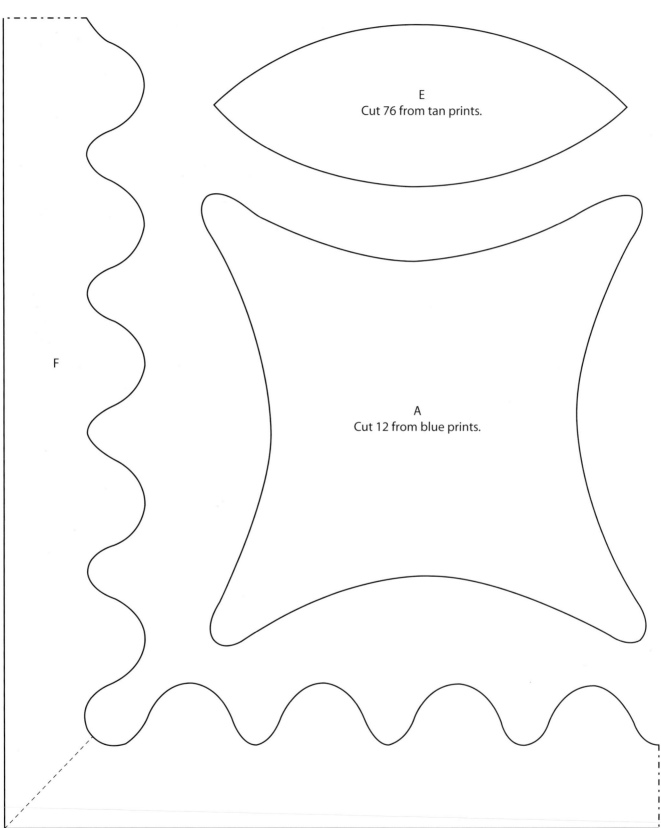

E
Cut 76 from tan prints.

F

A
Cut 12 from blue prints.

ROSE OF SHARON

Rose of Sharon, hand appliquéd and hand quilted by Bobbi Finley, San Jose, California, 1998–2001. 72½" × 72½".

Bobbi Finley found inspiration in a red-and-green quilt uncovered by the Kentucky Quilt Project. She updated the color scheme with complementary colors of yellow and purple and complemented the lively block with a border cleverly derived from the same design. Her appliqué designs of prints contrast with backgrounds of geometric woven plaids and stripes. The scalloped borders are a masterpiece of needle-turn technique. She added one more old-fashioned detail with a flat piping (or flange) inserted into the binding seams.

This is one of several Rose of Sharon quilts that Bobbi has made. The name comes from a Biblical metaphor in the Song of Solomon: "I am the rose of Sharon, and the lily of the valleys" (Solomon 2:1).

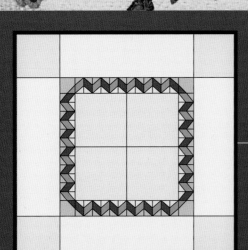

QUILT SIZE: 72½″ × 72½″

BLOCK SIZE: 18″ × 18″

BORDER WIDTHS: 5¼″, 13″

YOU NEED:

4 appliquéd blocks
Pieced inner border
Appliquéd outer border

FABRIC REQUIREMENTS

Medium yellow plaid for block backgrounds and borders: 2½ yards

Light yellow plaid for outer borders: 2¾ yards

Bright yellow print for appliqué pieces: ¼ yard

2 medium purple prints for appliqué pieces: ½ yard each

2 bright red (magenta or fuchsia) prints for appliqué pieces: ½ yard each

Dark purple print for appliqué pieces: ½ yard

8 different greens for appliqué pieces: ¼ yard each

Gold stripe for borders: 1⅜ yards

Dark purple plaid for borders and binding: 2⅛ yards

Medium purple plaid for inner borders and binding flange: 1¼ yards

Backing: 4½ yards

Batting: 77″ × 77″

CUTTING INSTRUCTIONS

Make templates for the patchwork and appliqué using the patterns on pages 39–40. For hand appliqué, add a scant ¼″ seam allowance.

From medium yellow plaid

Cut 4 squares 19½″ × 19½″ for block backgrounds. Trim to 18½″ × 18½″ after the appliqué is complete.

Cut 4 squares 13½″ × 13½″ for outer border corners.

Piece X: Cut 24 and 24 reversed for inner borders.

From light yellow plaid

Cut 4 lengthwise strips 13½″ × 47″ for outer borders.

From bright yellow print

Piece A: Cut 20 for blocks and 32 for borders.

From 5 purple and red prints

Piece B: Cut a total of 20 for blocks and 32 for borders.

Piece C: Cut a total of 20 for blocks and 32 for borders.

Piece F: Cut a total of 32 for blocks and 28 for borders.

From dark purple print

Piece D: Cut 4 for blocks and 8 for borders.

From 8 green prints

Piece E: Cut a total of 48 for blocks and 84 for borders.

Piece G: Cut a total of 32 for blocks and 28 for borders.

Bias strips for the stems and vines

Cut bias strips ½" wide. Fold under edges to make ¼" finished bias strips. You will need approximately 14 yards of bias to cut the following:

Piece H: Cut a total of 16 for blocks and 28 for borders.

Piece I: Cut 16 for blocks and 28 for borders. Use leftover pieces to make 16 straight stems for blocks.

From gold stripe

Cut 4 lengthwise strips 2¼" × 47" for appliquéd scallops for outer borders. Using pattern J, mark and cut scallops along 1 edge of each strip.

Piece K: Cut 4 for scallop corners.

Cut 4 squares 5¾" × 5¾". Measure 2⅞" on both sides of 1 corner of each square and trim at this measurement to make piece W for inner borders.

Piece X: Cut 24 and 24 reversed for inner borders.

From dark purple plaid

Cut 4 lengthwise strips 2¼" × 73" for appliquéd scallops in outer borders. Using pattern J, mark and cut scallops along 1 edge of each strip.

Note: The corner scallop is modified.

Cut 5 strips 2¼" × length of fabric for binding.

Cut 1 square 3⅝" × 3⅝"; cut in half diagonally to make 2 of piece V for inner borders.

Piece Y: Cut 24 for inner borders.

From medium purple plaid

Cut 1 square 3⅝" × 3⅝"; cut in half diagonally to make 2 of piece V for inner borders.

Piece Z (reverse piece Y): Cut 24 for inner borders.

Cut 1" bias strips to total 8½ yards long for binding flange.

SEWING INSTRUCTIONS

Appliquéing the blocks

Prepare the appliqué pieces using your favorite method.

Arrange the pieces and baste, pin, or glue them in place. Vary the curves of the stems for a folk art look.

Stitch the pieces using your favorite method. Trim the blocks to 18½" × 18½."

Piecing the inner border

The pieced inner border is made up of rectangular blocks with square blocks in the corners.

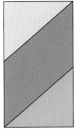

Inner border pieces

Stitch triangle piece V to the corner of piece W to make each corner square. Press. Make 4 corner squares, 2 with medium purple piece V and 2 with dark purple piece V.

Stitch triangle pieces X to the Y and Z parallelograms. Make sure the longer right angle side of each triangle is at the top and bottom of each block. Make 48 blocks of each fabric arrangement. Press.

Arrange and stitch together 12 blocks to make each inner border. Press.

Add a corner square to each end of 2 border pieces to make the top and bottom borders. Press.

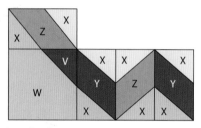

Inner border arrangement

Appliquéing the outer border

Sew the medium yellow plaid border corner pieces to the ends of 2 border pieces to make the top and bottom borders. Press.

Baste a gold stripe scalloped piece to the inside edge of each border by stitching a basting line (hand or machine) ⅛″ from the straight edge.

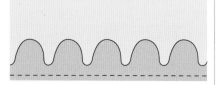

Baste straight edge

Stitch the curved edges using your favorite technique. Stitch the gold stripe corner piece (K) to each corner square.

Arrange the appliqué pieces on the borders and baste, pin, or glue in place.

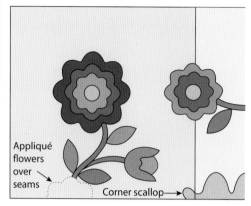

Appliqué flowers over seams

Corner scallop

Border corner

Note: The appliqué pieces at the ends of the side borders will be added after the borders are sewn to the quilt.

SETTING THE QUILT

Make 2 rows of 2 blocks each. Join the rows. Press.

Add the side inner borders. Press.

Add the top and bottom inner borders. Press.

Add the side outer borders. Press.

Add the top and bottom outer borders. Press.

Finish stitching the flowers over the seams.

Add the dark purple scallop pieces to the outer edges, in the same manner that you added the gold stripe scallop pieces.

BINDING

Join the ends of the medium purple plaid bias strips to make 1 long strip. Press the strip in half lengthwise.

Bind the quilt in your favorite fashion, inserting the purple plaid bias strip as a flat piping or flange.

Layer the folded flange on top of the folded binding, raw edges even. Sew the binding on as you would usually do, catching the raw edges of the flange in that seam.

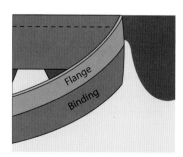

Flange

Binding

Sew flange with binding.

QUILTING

Bobbi echo quilted each appliqué shape to add dimension. She quilted parallel diagonal lines ½″ apart behind the appliqué. In the blocks, these lines form a square on point where they meet on the seams. She echo quilted the scallops and the zigzag pieces.

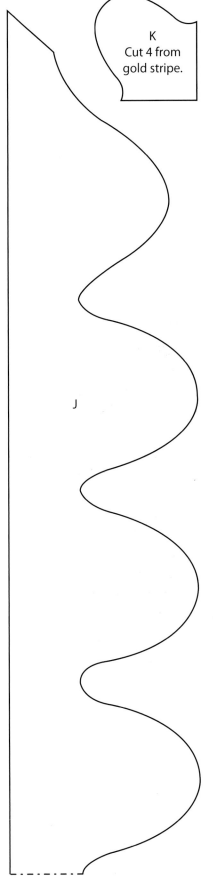

K
Cut 4 from gold stripe.

J

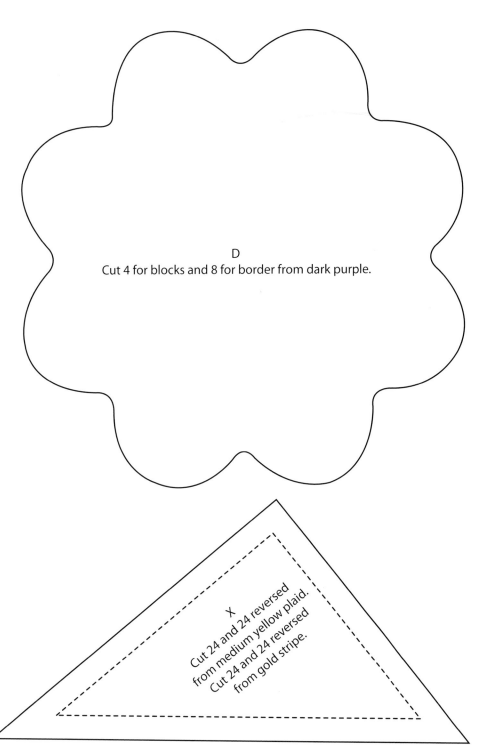

D
Cut 4 for blocks and 8 for border from dark purple.

X
Cut 24 and 24 reversed from medium yellow plaid. Cut 24 and 24 reversed from gold stripe.

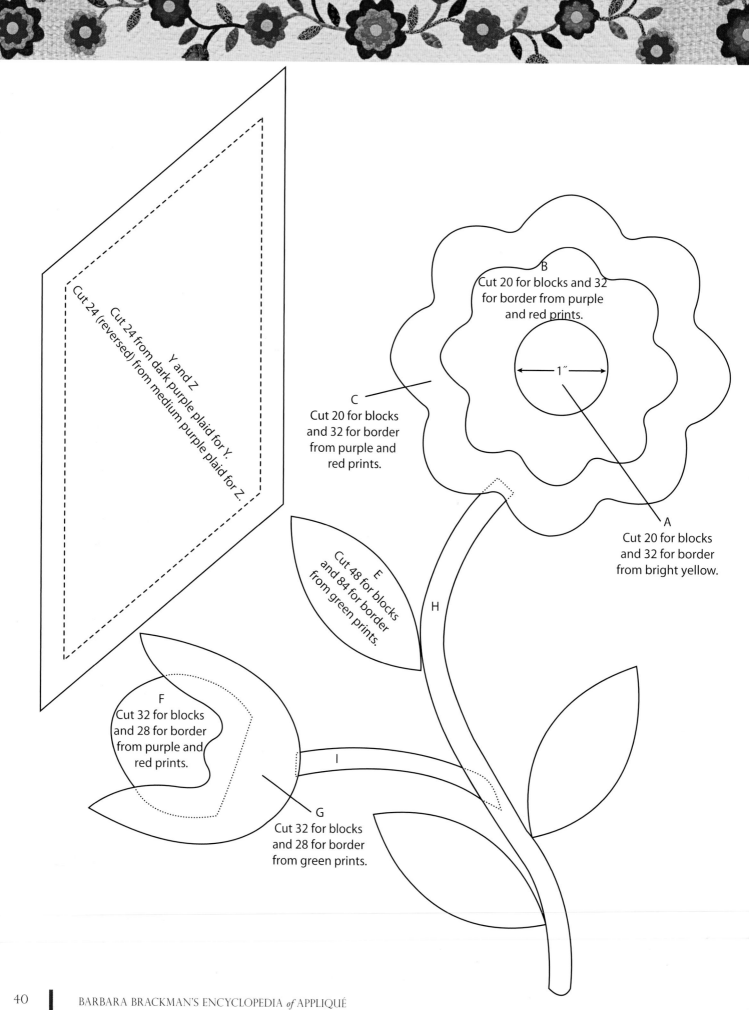

Y and Z
Cut 24 from dark purple plaid for Y.
Cut 24 (reversed) from medium purple plaid for Z.

B
Cut 20 for blocks and 32
for border from purple
and red prints.

1″

C
Cut 20 for blocks
and 32 for border
from purple and
red prints.

A
Cut 20 for blocks
and 32 for border
from bright yellow.

E
Cut 48 for blocks
and 84 for border
from green prints.

H

F
Cut 32 for blocks
and 28 for border
from purple and
red prints.

I

G
Cut 32 for blocks
and 28 for border
from green prints.

LANCASTER FOLK FEATHERS

Lancaster Folk Feathers, by Connie J. Nordstrom, Farmington, New Mexico, 2006. 26″ × 26.″

Connie Nordstrom loves to make miniature versions of antique appliqué. Here she's used a color scheme popular in Lancaster County, Pennsylvania, to reproduce an antique design full of bright color. This variation of the pattern we usually call Princess Feather is based on a rotational repeat of six units (see page 116) rather than the more common eight. For the background, Connie used a double pink reproduction print. She also used a reproduc-

tion Turkey red plain fabric for the appliqué. The green pieces in the quilt are from a single-shaded green fabric.

Connie backs her appliqué fabric with a thin fusible web to keep it from fraying and does not add seam allowances when she cuts. She machine stitches the raw edges with a tiny stitch that defines the edge with a fine line.

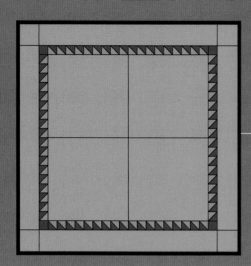

QUILT SIZE: 26″ × 26″

BLOCK SIZE: 9″ × 9″

BORDER WIDTHS: 1″, 3″

YOU NEED:

4 appliquéd blocks

Pieced inner border

Plain outer border

FABRIC REQUIREMENTS

Pink print for block backgrounds and outer borders: ¾ yard

Red for appliqué pieces and inner borders: ½ yard

Blue for appliqué pieces, inner borders, and binding: ⅝ yard

Gold for appliqué pieces: ¼ yard

Green for appliqué pieces: ½ yard

Backing: ⅞ yard

Batting: 30″ × 30″

CUTTING INSTRUCTIONS

Cut the appliqué pieces using the patterns on page 44. For hand appliqué, add a scant ¼″ seam allowance.

From pink print

Cut 4 squares 10½″ × 10½″ for block backgrounds. Trim to 9½″ × 9½″ after the appliqué is complete.

Cut 4 strips 3½″ × 20½″ for outer borders.

Cut 4 squares 3½″ × 3½″ for outer border corners.

From red

Piece A: Cut 4.

Piece G: Cut 24.

Cut 4 squares 1½″ × 1½″ for inner border corners.

Cut 3 strips 2½″ × width of fabric; subcut into 36 squares 2½″ × 2½″ and cut in half diagonally to make oversized pieces for paper-pieced inner borders.

From blue

B: Cut 4.

H: Cut 24.

Cut 3 strips 2½″ × width of fabric; subcut into 36 squares 2½″ × 2½″ and cut in half diagonally to make oversized pieces for paper-pieced inner borders.

Cut 3 strips 2¼″ × width of fabric for binding.

From gold

Piece C: Cut 4.

Piece F: Cut 24.

From green

Piece D: Cut 24.

Piece E: Cut 24.

SEWING INSTRUCTIONS

Appliquéing the blocks

Prepare the appliqué pieces using your favorite method.

Arrange the pieces and baste, pin, or glue them in place.

Rotate the 6 feathers and 6 iris stems as shown. Vary the curves of the stems for a folk art look.

Stitch the pieces using your favorite technique. Trim the blocks to 9½″ × 9½″.

Piecing the inner border

Copy the paper piecing pattern 8 times. Position the fabrics on the blank side of the paper and stitch on the printed side.

Begin with a blue oversized triangle. Hold the pattern and fabric up to the

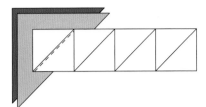

light and position the fabric right side up so it completely covers the triangle and extends at least ¼″ beyond the printed lines. Pin it in place.

Place a red oversized triangle right side down on top of the first fabric. Stitch on the line.

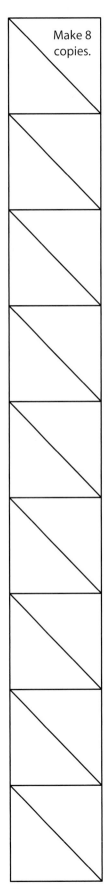

Make 8 copies.

Stitch on line.

Trim the seam allowances to ¼″. Open and press.

Continue adding triangles, alternating the blue and red fabrics, until you have covered the entire pattern. Trim the seam allowances around the outside edge of the pattern to ¼″.

Make 8 pieces. Sew 2 pieces together to make each of 4 inner borders. Remove the paper patterns.

SETTING THE QUILT

Make 2 rows of 2 blocks each. Join the rows. Press.

Add the side inner borders. Press.

Sew a red square to each end of the top and bottom inner borders. Press.

Add the top and bottom inner borders. Press.

Add the side outer borders. Press.

Sew the corner squares to each end of the top and bottom outer borders. Press.

Add the top and bottom outer borders. Press.

QUILTING

Connie machine quilted by echoing the larger appliqué shapes ¼″ inside the patch and stitched around each triangle close to the seamline in the ditch. She quilted small wreaths or parts of wreaths where the block seams meet. She quilted a close meander around the appliqué in the blocks. In the border, she created a swag shape and filled in around it with a close meander stitch.

Paper piecing pattern

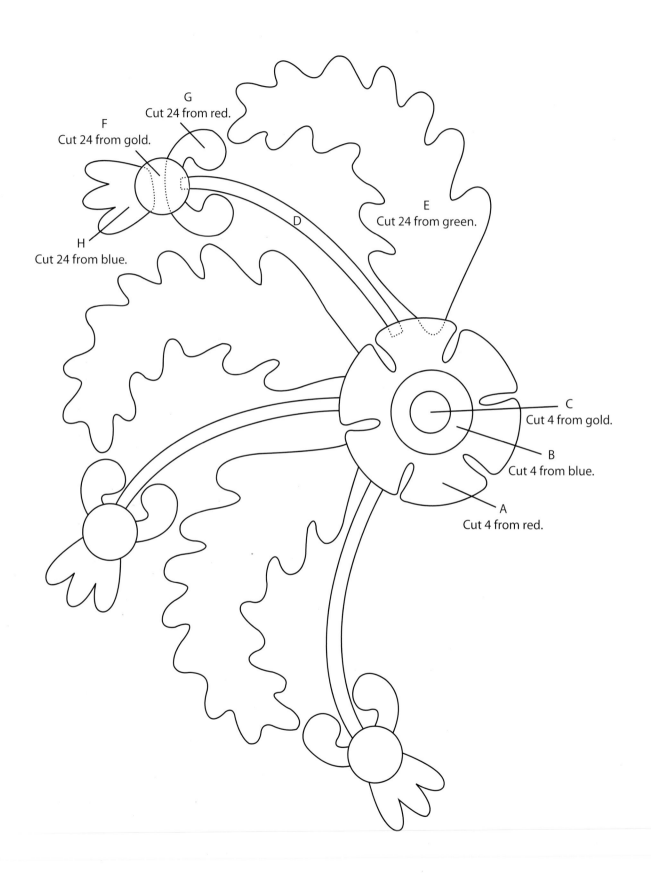

G
Cut 24 from red.

F
Cut 24 from gold.

E
Cut 24 from green.

D

H
Cut 24 from blue.

C
Cut 4 from gold.

B
Cut 4 from blue.

A
Cut 4 from red.

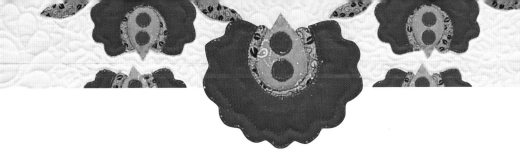

POT OF FLOWERS

Pot of Flowers, by Connie J. Nordstrom, Farmington, New Mexico, 1999. 26″ × 26″.

Connie Nordstrom's inspiration for this classic red-and-green miniature was a four-block quilt made using the floral urn pictured in the index as 41.52. Her updates include the tiny red inner border to frame the blocks.

Connie stabilizes her fabric with a fusible web and does not add seam allowances for her machine appliqué over raw edges.

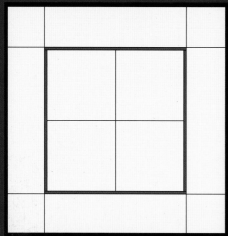

QUILT SIZE: 26″ × 26″

BLOCK SIZE: 8″ × 8″

BORDER WIDTHS: ¼″, 4¾″

YOU NEED:

4 appliquéd blocks

Plain inner border

Appliquéd outer border

FABRIC REQUIREMENTS

Ivory for block backgrounds, outer borders, and binding: 1 yard

Turkey red plain reproduction for appliqué pieces and inner borders: ½ yard

Green for appliqué pieces: ½ yard

Gold for appliqué pieces: ¼ yard

Dark green for appliqué pieces: ½ yard

Backing: ⅞ yard

Batting: 30″ × 30″

CUTTING INSTRUCTIONS

Cut the appliqué pieces using the patterns on pages 47–48. For hand appliqué, add a scant ¼″ seam allowance.

From ivory

Cut 4 squares 9½″ × 9½″ for block backgrounds. Trim to 8½″ x 8½″ after the appliqué is complete.

Cut 4 strips 5¼″ × 17″ for outer borders.

Cut 4 squares 5¼″ × 5¼″ for outer border corners.

Cut 3 strips 2¼″ × width of fabric for binding.

From red

Cut 2 strips ¾″ × 16½″ for side inner borders.

Cut 2 strips ¾″ × 17″ for top and bottom inner borders.

Piece A: Cut 12.

Piece D: Cut 24.

Piece I: Cut 4.

Piece K: Cut 4.

Piece N: Cut 32.

From green

Piece B: Cut 12.

Piece E: Cut 4 and 4 reversed.

Piece F: Cut 4.

Piece G: Cut 4 and 4 reversed.

Piece H: Cut 4 and 4 reversed.

From gold

Piece C: Cut 12.

Piece N: Cut 16.

From dark green

Piece J: Cut 4 (cut each as 1 piece).

Piece L: Cut 12.

Piece M: Cut 4.

SEWING INSTRUCTIONS

Appliquéing the blocks

Press the backgrounds into quarters diagonally, vertically, and horizontally to create lines for placement.

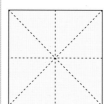

Placement lines

Prepare the appliqué pieces using your favorite method.

Arrange the pieces and baste, pin, or glue them in place.

Position piece B first, then build the flowers by adding pieces A, C, and D on top.

Position piece K on top of piece J.

Stitch the pieces using your favorite technique. Trim the blocks to 8½″ × 8½″.

Appliquéing the outer borders

Prepare the appliqué pieces using your favorite method.

Arrange the pieces and baste, pin, or glue them in place.

 Note: The corner appliqué pieces will be added after the borders are sewn to the quilt.

Stitch the pieces using your favorite technique.

SETTING THE QUILT

Make 2 rows of 2 blocks each. Join the rows. Press.

Add the side inner borders. Press.

Add the top and bottom inner borders. Press.

Add the side outer borders. Press.

Sew the corner squares to the ends of the top and bottom outer borders. Press.

Add the top and bottom outer borders. Press.

Finish the appliqué pieces in the corners.

QUILTING

Connie machine quilted by echoing the larger appliqué shapes ¼″ inside the patch. She quilted small wreaths or parts of wreaths where the block seams meet. She quilted a close meander around the appliqué in the blocks, added a diagonal grid about ¾″ apart in the border above the swag, and echoed the swag below.

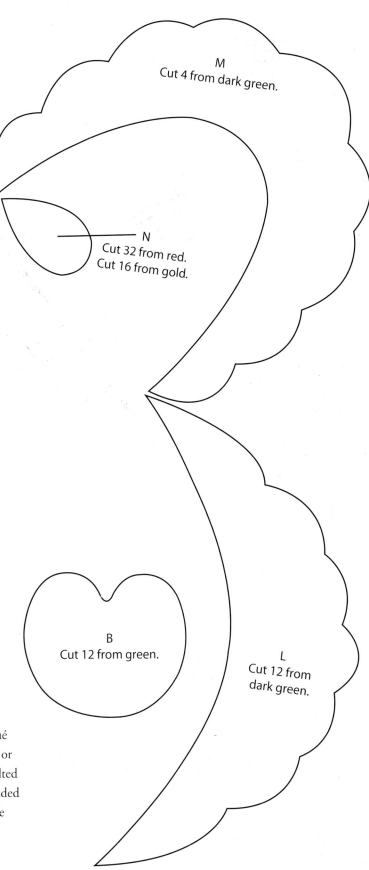

M
Cut 4 from dark green.

N
Cut 32 from red.
Cut 16 from gold.

B
Cut 12 from green.

L
Cut 12 from dark green.

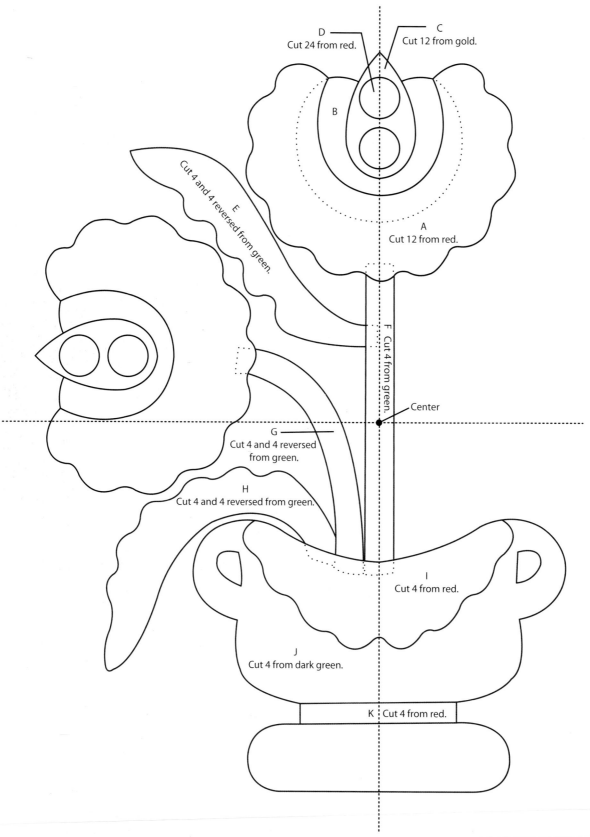

D
Cut 24 from red.

C
Cut 12 from gold.

B

A
Cut 12 from red.

E
Cut 4 and 4 reversed from green.

F Cut 4 from green.

Center

G
Cut 4 and 4 reversed
from green.

H
Cut 4 and 4 reversed from green.

I
Cut 4 from red.

J
Cut 4 from dark green.

K   Cut 4 from red.

Chapter 2

the INDEX

The patterns are indexed by design rather than name so you can find an unnamed pattern. The Key to Major Categories, which follows, will direct you to a specific area, where another key will help you find the page with your pattern. Appliqué's diversity dictates an approach to classification different from that used for pieced designs. Rather than looking for an exact match to an unknown appliqué pattern, you must try to fit it into a class of designs.

I have grouped the designs into numerous classes, generally based on the geometry of each design. Many nineteenth-century patterns, for example, are symmetrical, with a four-way, mirror-image balance. (If a cross were drawn north to south and east to west across the design, the four corners would be identical.) I began the index with these symmetrical patterns, which are further classified into the following general categories: wreaths (*Wreaths*), repeats of four elements radiating from the center (*Four Elements*), repeats of eight identical elements radiating from the center (*Eight Elements*), eight repeats with four of one element and four of another alternating around a center (*Four Plus Four Elements*), repeats

with nothing in the center (*Corner Designs*), and repeats of *More Than Eight Elements*.

Patterns with different symmetries follow these. Basket designs, for example, usually have two-way mirror-image symmetry (only a single line divides them into equal halves). They are classified as *Containers* under *Other Symmetries*.

Animals, which are usually shown in profile, have no symmetry in the quilt block. You cannot draw a line and find a mirror image of the design. These are also classified as *Other Symmetries* and are found toward the end of that category. There are numerous categories and subcategories in this *Other Symmetry* section; most are pictorial and rather easy to find. Some twentieth-century blocks were designed to be arranged as a series, or a group of similar designs with a theme. These are classified as *Series*, followed by *Medallions*, which have a central design focus often surrounded by a series of borders. There is also a small category of *Strips*, in which the design is set together in linear fashion, rather than as blocks. Last is a small category of *Sash and Block Designs*, which includes blocks that require a certain patchwork sashing to make the pattern.

Each pattern is numbered with a decimal system. Basic numbers range from 1 to 100 followed by a decimal point. (Numbers beyond 100 have been assigned to pieced patterns in my previously published *Encyclopedia of Pieced Quilt Patterns*). If you plan to create a computerized database with this numbering system, please read the note at the end of this section concerning the numbers.

Some of the patterns could be pieced or are partially pieced and appliquéd. If I indexed them in the *Encyclopedia of Pieced Quilt Patterns*, I have provided a numeric cross-reference. I have also cross-referenced patterns within the *Encyclopedia of Appliqué*.

The letters "T" or "D" accompany each pattern. T means the design is, in my opinion, a traditional nineteenth-century pattern; D means it is likely a design that originated in a twentieth-century designer's studio. Occasionally, a pattern's origins are not obvious, and I have left a blank.

The pattern names are followed by a source (in some cases I had only a clipping with no source and in other cases—I confess—I forgot to write it down). The source is either an actual quilt in that pattern or a published source for the name and design. To find out more about the published source, read the references that follow the numerical index.

When several sources give the same name for a pattern, I have given you only the earliest source. For example, if the Ladies Art Company's catalog and Marguerite Ickis gave the same name for a design, I have listed the Ladies Art Company as the source because its nineteenth-century catalog predates Ickis's 1949 book. When several sources published the same design with different names, I have listed them in chronological order. The first name for each design is the oldest name I could find in print. An alphabetic index at the end can help you find the pattern if you know its name.

A NOTE ABOUT THE NUMBERS

One use for my numerical indexes is to communicate about pattern by number. I wish I could say that every appliqué design now has an "official" number, but this is not the case. Appliqué is too spontaneous to become official. My intent is to create a numbering system that also applies to unknown patterns. The number before the decimal point is unique to a specific category. Overall Boys, for example, are numbered 48, with individual designs having different decimal numbers. If you find an Overall Boy that is unlisted, you can do one of two things: (1) Give the pattern a decimal number that I haven't used. Start with 48 and give it one of the 999 possible decimal numbers. I have used only 16. (2) Call all unknown Overall Boys 48.000.

The patterns are indexed with a two-digit number plus decimal places up to three. When setting up a digital file for these numbers, make room for two digits and three decimal places. You may want to coordinate this file with my *Encyclopedia of Pieced Quilt Patterns*, which uses numbers from 111 to 9999. You'll need then to create space for four digits before the decimal and three after; all numbers are entered as seven digits. Thus, a wreath numbered 1.31 here should be entered as 0001.310.

KEY TO MAJOR CATEGORIES

Go through the descriptions below in order, beginning with #1.

1.

❖ If the design is organized in blocks, go to Step 2, below.

❖ If the design is organized into strips, see Strips (patterns numbered 90).

❖ If the design is organized around a central image, see Medallions (patterns numbered 80). Check the outline for subcategories.

2.

❖ If the blocks are identical, go to Step 3, below.

❖ If the blocks are a series (a twentieth-century designer pattern, with each block a variation of a theme), see Series (patterns numbered 70). Check the outline for subcategories.

❖ If the blocks are a sampler of different patterns, then each block will have to be identified separately. Go to Step 3, below.

3.

❖ If the block is a full wreath, see Wreaths (patterns numbered 1–4). Check the outline for subcategories.

❖ If the block is an open wreath, go to Leaves and Open Wreaths (patterns numbered 43).

❖ If the block is not a wreath, go to Step 4, below.

4.

❖ If the block design is a four-way symmetrical repeat (if when folded in quarters, the quarters are essentially identical), go to Step 5, below.

❖ If the block design is asymmetrical or has two-way symmetry (if when folded in half, the halves are essentially identical), go to Step 7 below.

5.

❖ If the symmetrical pattern radiates from a central design, go to Step 6, below.

❖ If the symmetrical pattern is empty in the center, see Corner Designs (patterns numbered 26).

6.

❖ If the central design has four identical radiating motifs, see Four Elements (patterns numbered 5–13). Check the outline for subcategories.

❖ If the central design has eight identical radiating motifs, see Eight Elements (patterns numbered 14–15). Check the outline for subcategories.

❖ If the central design has eight radiating motifs—four of one motif, four of another—see Four Plus Four Elements (patterns numbered 16–25). Check the outline for subcategories.

❖ If the central design has more than eight radiating motifs, see More Than Eight Elements (patterns numbered 27).

7.

Go through the list below and choose the first description that applies to your pattern.

❖ If the design is based on a repeat of five elements or has flowers with five petals, see Five Elements (patterns numbered 34–35).

❖ If the design is based on a repeat of six radiating motifs or has flowers with six petals, see Six Petals (patterns number 36).

❖ If the design has seven radiating motifs, see Seven Elements (patterns numbered 36.9).

❖ If the design is a floral bouquet in a basket, pot, bowl, and so forth, see Containers (patterns numbered 38–42). Check the outline for subcategories.

❖ If the design is a floral bouquet without a container, see Bouquets (patterns numbered 28–37). Check the outline for subcategories.

❖ If the design is a leaf, see Leaves and Open Wreaths (patterns numbered 43).

❖ If the design is an open wreath, see Leaves and Open Wreaths (patterns numbered 43).

❖ If the design is a floral tree, see Floral Trees (patterns numbered 44).

❖ If the design is a fruit or vegetable, see Fruits and Vegetables (patterns numbered 46).

❖ If the design does not have four-way symmetry and is not in the above categories, see Other Symmetries—Miscellaneous (patterns numbered 45).

❖ If the picture represents a person, see Human Figures (patterns numbered 47–50). Check the outline for subcategories.

❖ If the picture is an animal, insect, object, or symbol, see the patterns numbered 51–60. Check the outline for subcategories.

FOUR-WAY SYMMETRY 1–27

Wreaths 1–4

Leaves, Fruit, and Miscellaneous 1

Floral 2–4

Four Elements 5–13

Four Leaves 5

Four Fleurs-de-Lis 6

Four Buds 7

Four Tulips 8

Four Flowers, Fruit, and
Miscellaneous 9

Four Hearts 9.8

Four Miscellaneous Elements 9.9

Floral Centers, Four Elements 10-13

Eight Elements 14–15

Miscellaneous 14

Princess Feathers 15

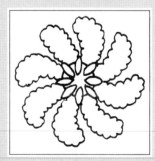

Four Plus Four Elements 16–25

Fruit 16

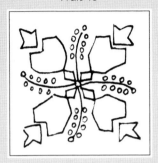

Reels 17

Combs 18

Miscellaneous 19–25

Corner Designs 26

More Than Eight Elements 27

OTHER SYMMETRIES 28–69

Bouquets 28–35

Tulips 28–30

Central Rose of Sharon 31

Miscellaneous 32–33

Five Elements or Five-Lobed Flowers 34–35

Six Petals or Six Elements 36

Stars and Roses 37.1–37.2

Water Lilies 37.3

Irises 37.7

Pots, Baskets, and Vases 39–42

Morning Glories 37.4

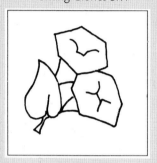

Daffodils 37.8

Leaves and Open Wreaths 43

Poppies 37.5

Daisies, Dahlias, and Sunflowers 37.9

Floral Trees 44

Pansies 37.6

Containers 38–42

Cornucopia 38

Miscellaneous 45

Fruits and Vegetables 46

Human Figures 47–49

Sunbonnet Girls and Colonial
Ladies 47

Overall Boys 48

Costumed Figures 49

Miscellaneous 50

Butterflies 51

Birds 52–54

Poultry 53

Eagles 54

Dogs 55

Cats, Rabbits, Fish, and So On 56

Trees 57

Houses and Buildings 58

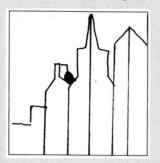

Boats 59

Symbols and Objects 60

SERIES 71–75

Leaves 71

Bouquets 72

Containers, Fruit, and Wreaths 73

Human Figures 74

Objects and Animals 75

MEDALLIONS 80–89

Floral Containers 80

Wreaths 81

Bouquets and Florals 82–83

Miscellaneous 84

Human Figures 85

Animals 86

Patriotic 87

Leaves and Trees 88

Miscellaneous Pictorial 89

STRIPS 90

Sash and Block 91

the INDEX *to* TRADITIONAL *and* MODERN APPLIQUÉ PATTERNS

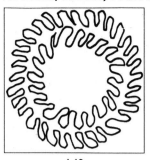

1.12
T* Unnamed—
Finley

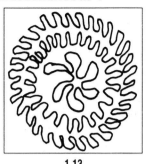

1.13
T Feather Crown—
Finley
T Feather Crown with a Ragged Robin
Center—
Hall and Kretsinger

1.21
Wreath of Leaves—
Boag kit

1.22
T Unnamed—
from an album dated 1857

1.26
T Foliage Wreath—
Ickis, pg. 61

1.27
T Wreath of Strawberry Leaves—
Sienkiewicz

1.28
T Unnamed—
from an album in Finley

1.31
D* Rose Garland—
Nancy Cabot, *Chicago Tribune* 1947

1.26
T Foliage Wreath—
Ickis, pg. 61

1.33
T Wreath of Cherries—
Comfort

1.34
T Cherry Wreaths—
from a quilt ca. 1860 in Orlofsky,
fig. 70

1.35
T Wreath of Cherries—
Sienkiewicz

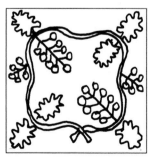

1.37
D* Primrose—
Aunt Martha Studios
Bridal Wreath—
Herrschners kit

1.4
T Bachelor's Dream—Irwin
Vase of Roses and
Cherries—Bresenhan/Texas
Quilts of Tennessee found several
examples in Tennessee

1.51
T Wreath of Grapes—
Ickis

1.55
Holly Wreath—
Nancy Cabot, *Chicago Tribune*

1.56
Muscatel Grape—
Boag kit

* T = Traditional nineteenth-century pattern   *** D** = Twentieth-century design studio pattern

Wreaths/Leaves, Fruit and Miscellaneous 1

1.57
T Grapes—
Nancy Cabot, *Chicago Tribune* 1935

1.62
D Rose Garland—
Nancy Cabot, *Chicago Tribune* 1947

1.64
D Garland of Leaves—
Nancy Cabot, *Chicago Tribune* 1933

1.65
D Bridal Wreath—
Ickis, pg. 118

1.67
D Brenda's Rosebud Wreath—
Sienkiewicz

1.69
D Pilot's Wheel—
Rural New Yorker

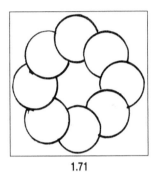

1.71
D Unnamed—
Wheeler/Brooks

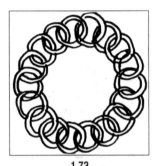

1.73
T Unnamed—
From an album dated 1848

Wreaths/Floral 2–4

1.76
T Unnamed—
alternates with a Democrat Rose in
Whitehill quilt at Denver Art Museum

2.13
T Grape Wreath—
name inscribed on quilt ca. 1870
Shelburne #10.323

2.16
T Wreath of Roses—
name inscribed on quilt ca. 1870
Shelburne #10.323

2.18
D Sweet Pea Wreath—
Nancy Cabot, *Chicago Tribune*

2.23
T Rose Wreath—
Ladies Art Company #262

2.24
T Flower Wreath—
Grandmother Clark Book 23

2.31
T Conventional Rose Wreath—Webster
Wreath of Roses—Webster
Rose Wreath—Aunt Martha Studios
Kentucky Rose—Finley

2.32
T The Garden Wreath—
Finley

2.33
T North Carolina Rose—
Aunt Martha 1933

2.34
T Dahlia Wreath—
Hall and Kretsinger pg. 171

2.36
T Wreath of Roses—
Ladies Art Company #189

2.4
T Wreath of Roses—
Carlie Sexton

2.51
D Cluster of Roses—
Webster ca. 1925

2.53
D Hollyhock Wreath—
McKim ca. 1930 & Nancy Cabot,
Chicago Tribune 1933

2.55
T Wreath of Roses—
The Family 1913

2.57
T Wreath of Roses—
Rural New Yorker (note wreath is
not a circle)

2.61
T Wreath of Roses—
Ickis

2.62
T Wreath of Roses—
Hall and Kretsinger
Garden Wreath—
Hall and Kretsinger

2.63
T Kentucky Rose—
St. Louis Fancywork, Hall and
Kretsinger

2.64
T Rose of Heaven—
Nancy Cabot, *Chicago Tribune* 1934

2.65
T President's Wreath—
Hall and Kretsinger

2.66
T Martha Washington Wreath—
Rural New Yorker

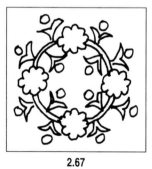

2.67
T Roses & Bells—
Nancy Cabot, *Chicago Tribune* 1935

2.68
T Unnamed—
Modern Priscilla, March, 1926

2.69
T Newark Wreath—
Nancy Cabot, *Chicago Tribune*

2.71
T The Rose Quilt—
Ladies Home Journal 1908

2.72
T President's Wreath—
Grandmother Clark

2.73
T Centennial Wreath—
Nancy Cabot, *Chicago Tribune* 1938

2.74
T Indian Paintbrush—
Finley

2.75
T Wreath of Roses—
Hearth and Home

2.76
T President's Wreath—
Finley, plate 27

2.77
T Bud and Rose Wreath—
Ickis, pg. 138

2.78
T Wild Rose Wreath—
Ickis, pg. 66

3.1
D Wreath—
Nancy Cabot, *Chicago Tribune* 1936

3.2
D Moonflower—
Nancy Cabot, *Chicago Tribune* 1934

3.31
T Dahlia Wreath—
Nancy Cabot, *Chicago Tribune* 1933

3.32
T Wreath of Carnations—
Hall and Kretsinger, pg. 124

3.33
T Wreath of Roses—
The Family 1913

3.34
T Dahlia Wreath—
name inscribed on a quilt ca. 1870
Shelburne #10.323

3.5
T Rose and Bud Wreath—
Ladies Art Company #6064
Rose Wreath—
Nancy Cabot, *Chicago Tribune*

3.36
T Wreath of Roses—
Hall and Kretsinger, pg. 149

3.37
T Unnamed—
from an album dated 1850

3.42
T Rose Wreath—
Nancy Cabot, *Chicago Tribune*

3.43
T Unnamed—
Prudence Penny

3.48
T Unnamed—
Clark/Ohio

3.5
T Wreath of Wild Roses—
Hall and Kretsinger

3.63
T Iowa Rose—
Carlie Sexton

3.64
T Wreath of Pansies—
Hall and Kretsinger pg. 184
(mislabeled; should have read Iowa
Rose Wreath)

3.7
T Iowa Rose—
Nancy Cabot, *Chicago Tribune* 1933
D Des Moines Rose—
Nancy Cabot, *Chicago Tribune* 1937

3.83
T Unnamed—
from an album dated 1851

3.84
T Fleur-de-lis with Folded Rose
Buds—
Sienkiewicz

3.92
D Tulip Circle—
Wheeler/Brooks

3.94
D Crocus Wreath—
Nancy Cabot, *Chicago Tribune* 1933

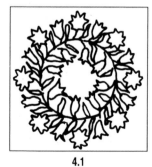

4.1
T Hawaiian Flower—
Nancy Cabot, *Chicago Tribune* 1935

4.21
D Tulip Time—
Hinson/Quilting Manual

4.25
T Strawberry Wreath—
name inscribed on quilt ca. 1870
Shelburne #10.323

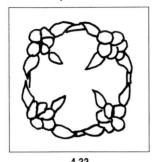

4.33

D Pansy Design—
Ladies Art Company #6065
Iowa Rose Wreath—Hall and Kretsinger.
Probably mislabeled; should have read
Wreath of Pansies.

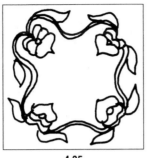

4.35

D Pansy—
Mrs. Danner

4.4

D Wild Rose Wreath—
Ladies Home Journal 8/1911

4.53

D Wreath of Morning Glories—
Comfort

4.55

D Morning Glory—
The Family 1913

4.6

Unnamed—
Clark/Ohio

4.72

T Victorian Rose—
quilt by Whitehill Denver Art
Museum

4.78

D Wreath of Roses—
Webster ca. 1925

4.81

T Unnamed—
from an album dated 1854

4.82

D Primrose Wreath—
Webster design ca. 1925

4.84

D Nasturtium Wreath—
Webster design ca. 1925

4.86

D Unnamed—
Aunt Martha/*Prize-Winning Quilts*
ca. 1933

4.87

D Lily Design—
Comfort

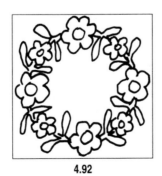

4.92

D Flower Wreath—
Nancy Cabot, *Chicago Tribune* 1934

4.94

D Wild Rose Wreath—
Rural New Yorker 1934

4.96

D Wreath of Daisies—
Nancy Cabot, *Chicago Tribune* 1933

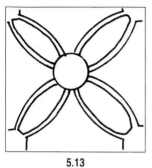

5.13
T Job's Tears—
Nancy Cabot, *Chicago Tribune*
1933. See as a pieced pattern
#3079

5.15
D Red Hot Poker—
Nancy Cabot, *Chicago Tribune* 1934
Pompom—
Nancy Cabot, *Chicago Tribune* 1937

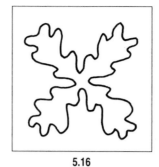

5.16
T Tobacco Leaf—
Nancy Cabot, *Chicago Tribune* 1933

5.17
T Unnamed—
from an album dated 1857. A
similar leaf alternated with a Double
Irish Chain block called Double Irish
Cross in *Country Life* 1923

5.18
D Block from the Leaf Quilt—
Nancy Page. See #71.5

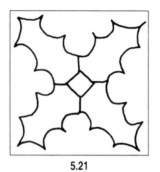

5.21
D Oak Leaves—
Nancy Cabot, *Chicago Tribune* 1937

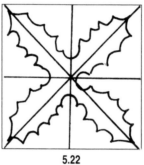

5.22
D Holly Leaves—
Nancy Cabot, *Chicago Tribune* 1936

5.24
T Tobacco Leaves—
Finley plate 59

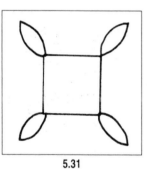

5.31
T Unnamed—
from a quilt ca. 1840

5.32
T Unnamed—
from a quilt ca. 1840

5.33
T Honey Bee—
Nancy Cabot, *Chicago Tribune* 1933
T Birds in the Air—
Coats and Clark 1942. See as
pieced patterns #2217-2218.

5.34
T Antique Fleur-de-lis—
Nancy Cabot, *Chicago Tribune* 1934

5.36
T Turkey Tracks—
Finley. See as a pieced pattern
#3109.
Wandering Foot—
Finley

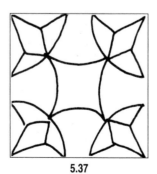

5.37
T The Swallow—
Rural New Yorker 1937
Burr and Thistle—
Rural New Yorker 1937. See pieced
patterns #3096-3109.

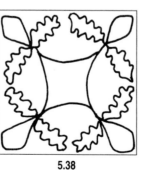

5.38
T Aunt Dinah's Delight—
Carlie Sexton

5.39
T Aunt Dinah's Delight—
Nancy Cabot, *Chicago Tribune*

5.42
T Conventional Tulip—
Farmer's Wife 10/1929

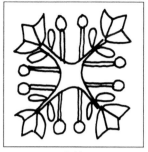

5.44
T Unnamed—
from a quilt in MacDowell/Michigan
pg. 53

5.45
T Unnamed—
from an album dated 1853

5.47
T Rose Leaf—
Rural New Yorker

5.49
T Amazon Lily—
Nancy Cabot, *Chicago Tribune* 1937

5.51
T Unnamed—
from an album dated 1847

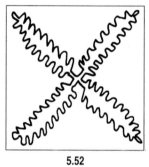

5.52
T Princess Feather—
Bresenhan/Texas

5.54
T Unnamed—
from an album dated 1844

5.55
T Laurel Leaves—
Shelburne Museum pg. 61

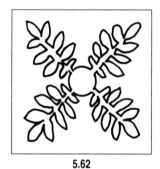

5.62
D Sumach Leaf—
block from the Leaf Quilt by Nancy
Page. See 71.5

5.63
T Unnamed—
from an album dated 1847

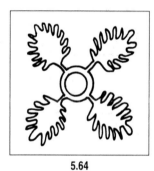

5.64
T Unnamed—
from an album dated 1851

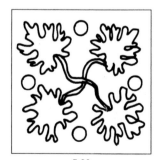

5.66
T Unnamed—
from an album dated 1856

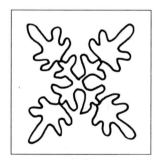

5.68
T Unnamed—
from an album dated 1855

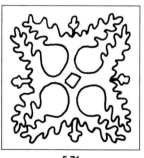

5.71
T Charter Oak—
Finley pg. 124

5.72
T Oak Leaf—
Farmer's Wife 1932

Four Leaves 5

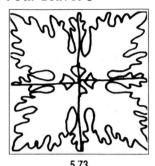

5.73
T Maple Leaf—
Ladies Art Company

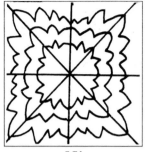

5.74
D Flame Block—
Nancy Cabot, *Chicago Tribune*
Flames—
Nancy Cabot, *Chicago Tribune* 1935

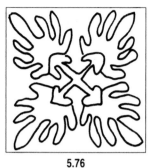

5.76
T Cotton Boll—
from a repeat block quilt, ca. 1860, in
Roberson/North Carolina
T Chrysanthemum—same source

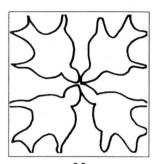

5.8
T Four Little Birds—
Ladies Art Company #303

Four Fleur-de-lis 6

5.93
D Arrowroot Block—
Nancy Cabot, *Chicago Tribune* 1935

5.94
D Tulip Square—
Nancy Cabot, *Chicago Tribune* 1936

6.1
T Poplar Leaf—
Ladies Art Company #111

6.2
T Philadelphia Beauty—
Ladies Art Company #116

6.3
T Four Frogs—
Ladies Art Company #283

6.4
T Washington Square—
Farm Journal 1/1934

6.5
T Bride's Fancy—
Hearth and Home
Winchester—
Hearth and Home

6.6
T Fleur de Lis—
McKim

Four Buds 7

6.7
T Lobster—
Hinson/*Quilting Manual* plate 22

6.8
D Friendship Plume—
Mountain Mist

7.2
T Orange Block—
Nancy Cabot, *Chicago Tribune* 1938

7.4
D Baby Rose—
Carlie Sexton

Four Buds 7   Four Tulips 8

7.6
D   Moon Blossoms—
Nancy Cabot, *Chicago Tribune* 1935

8.12
T   Lily of the Valley—
Nancy Cabot, *Chicago Tribune* 1934

8.14
T   Unnamed—
from a clipping ca. 1890

8.16
T   Four Tulips—
Ladies Art Company #453

8.18
T   Lily of the Valley—
Ladies Art Company #391

8.22
T   Tulip Tree Leaves—
Hall and Kretsinger

8.24
T   Tulip Tree Leaves—
Webster

8.33
T   Dutch Tulip—
Nancy Cabot, *Chicago Tribune* 1933

8.38
T   Tulip—
from a quilt ca. 1885, in
Roberson/North Carolina, pg. 72

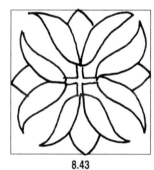

8.43
T   Four Tulips—
Hall and Kretsinger, pg. 122

8.47
D   Lombardy Lily—
Nancy Cabot, *Chicago Tribune* 1938

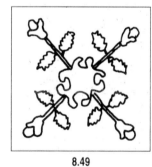

8.49
T   Unnamed—
from a quilt in Lasansky/Pieced,
plate 49

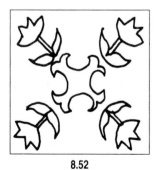

8.52
T   Summer Tulips—
Nancy Cabot, *Chicago Tribune* 1937

8.54
T   Tennessee Tulip—
McKim, *Patchwork Parade of States*

8.56
T   Conventional Tulips—
Rural New Yorker
Gay Tulips—
Needlecraft Magazine 1936

8.58
T   Colonial Patchwork—
Hearth and Home February, 1917

8.61
T Lotus Flower—
Hall and Kretsinger, pg 120

8.63
T Unnamed—
from a quilt, *Quilt Engagement
Calendar* 1977, plate 18

8.64
T Tulip—
from a quilt ca. 1935,
Roberson/North Carolina, pg. 76

8.65
T Tulip Crib Quilt—
Ickis, pg. 102

8.66
T Loretta's Rose—
Hall and Kretsinger, pg. 116

8.67
T Tulip—
Ladies Art Company #449

8.68
T Unnamed—
Aunt Martha, *Prize-Winning Quilts*

8.71
T Lotus Bud—
Hall and Kretsinger

8.73
T Indiana Rose—
Carlie Sexton

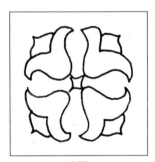

8.75
T Amaryllis—
Nancy Cabot, *Chicago Tribune* 1934
Scarlet Amaryllis—
Nancy Cabot, *Chicago Tribune* 1938

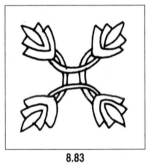

8.83
D Peony—
Ladies Art Company #6073

8.87
D Harebells—
Nancy Cabot, *Chicago Tribune* 1934

8.88
D St. Peter's Penny—
Nancy Cabot, *Chicago Tribune* 1934

8.92
T Golden Bells—
Nancy Cabot, *Chicago Tribune* 1936

8.94
T $200,000 Tulip—
Sienkeiwicz

8.95
T Unnamed—
from an album dated 1847

9.1
D Good Luck Clover—
Nancy Cabot, *Chicago Tribune* 1934

9.23
T Unnamed—
from an album dated 1854

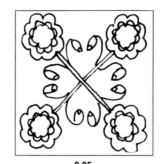

9.25
T Single Stem Rose Variation—
from a quilt ca. 1850,
Kimball pg. 146

9.26
T Original Rose—
Webster plate 51

9.28
T Unnamed—
from a quilt, *Quilt Engagement
Calendar* 1980, plate 56

9.32
T Grandmother's Dream—
Carlie Sexton, *Old Fashioned Quilts*
pg. 21

9.34
T Piney—
Carlie Sexton

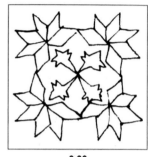

9.36
D Poinsettia—
Kansas City Star 1931

9.38
T Unnamed—
from an album dated 1852

9.41
D Curling Leaves—
Nancy Cabot, *Chicago Tribune* 1936

9.43
T Coxcomb—
from a quilt, ca.
1860, Clarke/*Kentucky* pg. 23

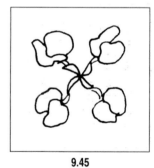

9.45
D Sweet Peas—
Mountain Mist

9.47
T Thistle Block—
Nancy Cabot, *Chicago Tribune* 1937

9.48
T Thistles—
Peto, *American Quilts*, pg. 63

9.52
D Magnolia Buds in Floral Maze—
Baroness Pignatoni in the
Minneapolis Morning Tribune

9.54
D Trumpet Vine Block—
Nancy Cabot, *Chicago Tribune*

Four Flowers, Fruit and Miscellaneous 9

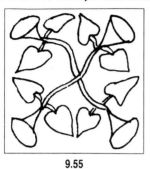

9.55
D Morning Glory—
Nancy Cabot, *Chicago Tribune* 1937

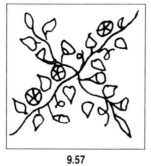

9.57
D Morning Glory—
Nancy Cabot, *Chicago Tribune* 1933

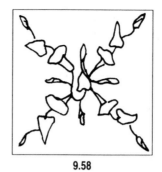

9.58
D Morning Glory—
Ladies Art Company

9.59
T Floral—
Spencer Museum of Art

Four Fruits 9.6–9.7

9.62
T Turquoise Berries—
Nancy Cabot, *Chicago Tribune* 1933

9.63
T Grapevine Block—
Nancy Cabot, *Chicago Tribune* 1937

9.67
T Pomegranate—
from a quilt in Havig/Missouri, pg. 34

9.68
T Cotton Boll—
from a quilt in Texas Heritage
Quilt Soc.

9.72
T Rosebuds—
Nancy Cabot, *Chicago Tribune*

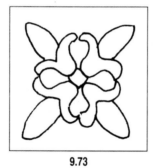

9.73
D Golden Corn—
Hall and Kretsinger, pg. 109

9.74
T Unnamed—
from an album dated 1854

9.75
T Pineapple—
Finley, plate 79

9.76
T Hawaiian Blocks—
Wheeler/Brooks #7053

9.77
T Hospitality—
Sienkeiwicz

9.78
T Unnamed—
from an album dated 1853

9.79
T Unnamed—
from an album dated 1855

9.812

T Mary Moore's Double Irish Chain —
Bureau Farmer 1930
Double Irish Cross—McKim. (both
alternated with a pieced Irish Chain
block; see as a pieced design #1017)

9.813

Unnamed—
Comfort September, 1928

9.821

T Good Luck Block—
Nancy Cabot, *Chicago Tribune* 1933
Luck Quilt—*Oklahoma Farmer
and Stockman* 1935
Four Leaf Clover—*Oklahoma Farmer and
Stockman* 1935 (all alternated with four patch,
see pieced design #1006)

9.822

T Good Luck Clover—
Needlecraft 1933

9.825

T Hearts—
unknown clipping ca. 1890

9.826

T Unnamed—
from an album dated 1857

9.83

T Roses and Hearts—
from a quilt ca. 1963, Marston and
Cunningham

9.842

T Eight of Hearts—
Nancy Cabot, *Chicago Tribune* 1933
Sweethearts—
Nancy Cabot, *Chicago Tribune*

9.843

T Double Heart—
unknown clipping ca. 1890
Friendship Quilt—
Ladies Art Company #180

9.844

T Traditional Geometric Design—
Ickis, pg. 47

9.85

T Hearts All Around—
Hearth and Home

9.874

Friendship Quilt—
Kansas City Star 1938
A Heart for Applique—
Kansas City Star 1951

9.875

Sweetheart Quilt—
Capper's Weekly

9.882

T Unnamed—
from an album dated 1854

9.884

T Unnamed—
from an album dated 1852

9.89

T Unnamed—
from an album dated 1850

9.912
D Dogwood Applique—
Farmer's Wife 1932
Forget Me Not—
Nancy Cabot, *Chicago Tribune* 1936

9.913
D Friendship Band—
Hearth and Home

9.921
D Double Poppy—
Nancy Cabot, *Chicago Tribune*

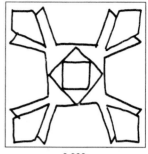

9.923
D Modern Corsage—
Nancy Cabot, *Chicago Tribune* 1936

9.924
D Flemish Tile—
Nancy Cabot, *Chicago Tribune* 1937

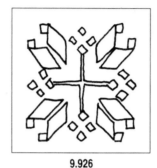

9.926
D Weathervane—
Nancy Cabot, *Chicago Tribune*

9.93
T Unnamed—
from an album dated 1860

9.941
D Four Chartres Lilies—
Nancy Cabot, *Chicago Tribune* 1936

9.943
D King's Crown—
Nancy Cabot, *Chicago Tribune* 1938

9.945
D Geneva Tassal Flower—
Nancy Cabot, *Chicago Tribune* 1936

9.95
D Rose and Lily Block—
Nancy Cabot, *Chicago Tribune* 1936

9.96
D Tipperary Tangle—
Nancy Cabot, *Chicago Tribune* 1935

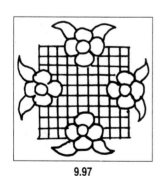

9.97
D Wild Roses and Squares—
Nancy Cabot, *Chicago Tribune* 1934

9.981
D Rock Rose—
Nancy Cabot, *Chicago Tribune* 1937

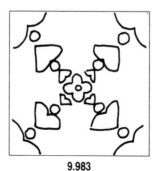

9.983
D Lilac Zinnia—
Nancy Cabot, *Chicago Tribune* 1936

9.99
T Whig Rose Variation—
from a quilt dated 1859 -
Crews/Nebraska

10.12
D Begonia—
Nancy Cabot, *Chicago Tribune* 1934

10.13
T Simple Floral Block—
Nancy Cabot, *Chicago Tribune*
Floral Block—
Nancy Cabot, *Chicago Tribune* 1937

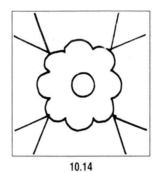

10.14
D Wild Rose Quilt—
Wheeler/Brooks #1974

10.16
D California Sunflower—
Ladies Art Company #459

10.22
T Peony and Buds—
Nancy Cabot, *Chicago Tribune* 1938

10.24
T French Rose—
Nancy Cabot, *Chicago Tribune*

10.32
D Star Flowers—
Nancy Cabot, *Chicago Tribune* 1935

10.35
D Daisy Block—
Nancy Cabot, *Chicago Tribune* 1937

10.37
D Rose Point—
Nancy Cabot, *Chicago Tribune* 1933

10.39
D Texas Sunflower—
Nancy Cabot, Grandmother Book
#29

10.42
T Original Rose #3—
Webster, figure 61

10.43
T Fringed Rose—
Nancy Cabot, *Chicago Tribune* 1935

10.52
T Rose of Sharon—
Herrschner
Wild Rose—
Mrs. Danner

10.53
T Open Dahlia—
name inscribed on a quilt ca. 1870
Shelburne #10.323

10.54
T Rose of Sharon—
McCall's Needlework Winter 1941–2

10.61
D Coneflower—
Nancy Cabot, *Chicago Tribune* 1934

10.63
T Unnamed—
from an album dated 1854

10.64
T Bleeding Heart—
Comfort

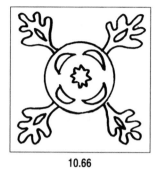

10.66
T Unnamed—
from an album dated 1853

10.67
T Charter Oak—
Hall and Kretsinger pg. 118

10.68
T Unnamed—
from an album dated 1845

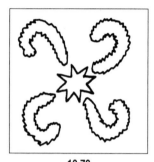

10.72
T Unnamed—
from an album dated 1863

10.74
T Unnamed—
alternates with Feathered Star in
Webster fig. 35

10.76
T Whirling Swastika—
Peto/*American Quilts* pg. 20

10.78
T Prince's Feather—
Mrs. Danner

10.82
D Royal Water Lily—
Nancy Cabot, *Chicago Tribune* 1934

10.83
D African Daisy—
Nancy Cabot, *Chicago Tribune* 1935

10.84
D Honeysuckle—
Nancy Cabot, *Chicago Tribune* 1934

10.85
D Dahlia—
Nancy Cabot, *Chicago Tribune* 1934

10.86
D Paneled Daisy—
Nancy Cabot, *Chicago Tribune* 1937

10.87
D Shasta Daisy—
Hearth and Home

10.89
T Fireworks—
Nancy Cabot, *Chicago Tribune* 1935
Midnight Sky—
Nancy Cabot, *Chicago Tribune* 1938

Floral Centers/Four Elements 10–13

11.12
T Hearts—
Shelburne Museum

11.15
T Unnamed—
from an album dated 1850

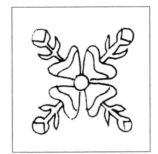

11.21
The Wild Rose—
Capper's Weekly
Conventional Wild Rose—
Hall and Kretsinger, pg. 116

11.22
Topeka Rose—
Hall and Kretsinger, pg. 111

11.23
Hearts and Flowers, Ickis, pg. 128

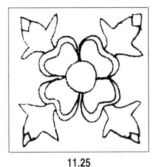

11.25
Ohio Rose—Carlie Sexton, Mountain
Mist, *Farmer's Wife* October, 1929
Rose of Sharon—*Capper's Weekly*
Yellow Rose of Texas—*Capper's Weekly*
Rose of Sharon—*Farmer's Wife* 1932

11.32
Rose of Sharon Cluster—
Ladies Art Company #6081

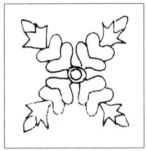

11.35
Rose of Sharon—
Hall and Kretsinger pg. 112

11.42
Colonial Rose—
St. Louis Fancy Work

11.45
Bud and Blossom—
The Family 1913

11.52
Prairie Rose—
Nancy Cabot, *Chicago Tribune*

11.55
Colonial Rose—
Sears, Roebuck and Co. 1934

11.62
Louisiana Rose—
Sears, Roebuck and Co. 1934

11.65
Ohio Rose—
Nancy Cabot, *Chicago Tribune* 1933

11.72
Radical Rose—
Hall and Kretsinger pg. 116

11.75
New Rose of Sharon—
Nancy Cabot, *Chicago Tribune* 1936

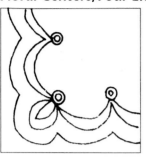

11.79b
The Rose of Sharon—
Mrs. Danner (scalloped edge)

11.25b
Yellow Rose of Texas—
Capper's Weekly

11.42b
Colonial Rose—
Louis Fancy Work

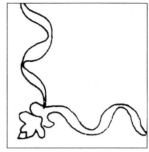

11.32b
Rose of Sharon Cluster—
Ladies Art Company #6081

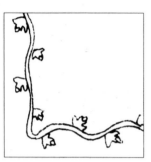

11.25b
Ohio Rose—
Mountain Mist

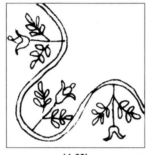

11.62b
Louisiana Rose—
Sears, Roebuck and Co. 1934

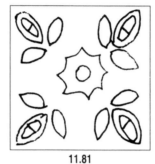

11.81
T Unnamed—
from an album dated 1850

11.82
T Unnamed—
from an album dated 1846

11.831
T Combination Rose—Webster
California Rose—Hall and
Kretsinger, pg. 114
Texas Yellow Rose—Hall and
Kretsinger, pg. 114

11.832
T Grandmother's Quilt—
St. Louis Fancywork

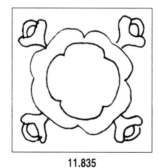

11.835
T Pennsylvania Dutch Rose—
Nancy Cabot, *Chicago Tribune* 1933

11.87
T From a quilt ca. 1850 in Safford
& Bishop, pg. 168

11.88
T Irish Rose—
Nancy Cabot, *Chicago Tribune* 1933

11.92
D New Tulip Block—
Nancy Cabot, *Chicago Tribune* 1936

11.95
D Tulips and Buds—
Nancy Cabot, *Chicago Tribune* 1937

11.97
T Unnamed—
from an album dated 1865

Floral Centers/Four Elements 10–13

12.12
T Rose Cross—
Hall and Kretsinger, pg. 104

12.14
T Rose and Lily—
Nancy Cabot, *Chicago Tribune* 1937
Unnamed—
Modern Priscilla March, 1926

12.18
T Rose Cross—
McKim

12.22
T Pomegranate—
Peto, *American Quilts* pg. 12

Four Tulips/Floral Center

12.14
T Jefferson Rose—
from a quilt ca. 1849 in
Ramsey/Tennessee, pg. 7 (Leaves
in corners are alternate blocks)

12.26
T Pomegranate—
Ladies Art Company #6018
Rose and Peony—
Farm and Fireside September, 1929

12.28
T Pomegranate—
Nancy Cabot, *Chicago Tribune* 1937

12.31
T Ohio Rose—
Hall and Kretsinger

12.33
T Scotch Thistle—
Carlie Sexton

12.35
Geranium Wreath—
Nancy Cabot, *Chicago Tribune* 1937

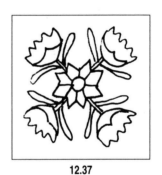

12.37
T Elderberry Bloom—
Nancy Cabot, *Chicago Tribune* 1938

12.39
T Spiced Pinks—
Nancy Cabot, *Chicago Tribune* 1937

12.41
T Ohio Rose—
Webster
Forget Me Not—
Carlie Sexton

12.42
T Ohio Rose—
Needlecraft Magazine 1926

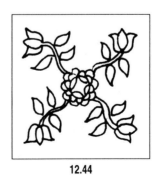

12.44
T Unnamed—
from a quilt in the *Quilt
Engagement Calendar* 1977, plate 2

12.47
D Cyclamen—
Nancy Cabot, *Chicago Tribune* 1935

12.52
T   Rose of 1840—
Nancy Cabot, *Chicago Tribune* 1935

12.55
D   Oriental Rose—
Nancy Cabot, *Chicago Tribune*

12.57
D   Persian Poinsettia—
Nancy Cabot, *Chicago Tribune* 1937

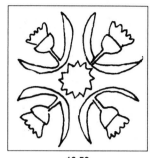

12.59
T   Thistle—
Nancy Cabot, *Chicago Tribune* 1937

12.62
T   Yellow Indiana Rose—
Nancy Cabot, *Chicago Tribune* 1938

12.63
T   Conventional Lily Applique—
Comfort September, 1928

12.65
T   Indiana Rose—
Nancy Cabot, *Chicago Tribune* 1933

12.68
T   Pumpkin—
Ladies Art Company #508

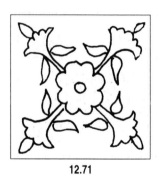

12.71
T   New Jersey Rose—
Nancy Cabot, *Chicago Tribune* 1933
Jersey Rose—
Nancy Cabot, *Chicago Tribune* 1937
Jersey Bouquet—
Nancy Cabot, *Chicago Tribune* 1937

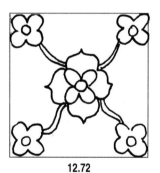

12.72
D   Memory Block—
Nancy Cabot, *Chicago Tribune* 1937

12.81
T   Unnamed—
from an album dated 1852

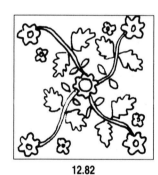

12.82
T   Unnamed—
from the center of a Cornucopia
from Mrs. Danner (see #38)

12.84
T   Democratic Rose—
Carlie Sexton

12.86
T   Unnamed—
from a quilt ca. 1840 in Safford and
Bishop, pg. 168

12.87
T   California Rose—
Bishop/Knopf, pg. 165

12.88
T   English Rose—
Hall and Kretsinger Page 22

Floral Centers/Four Elements 10–13

12.91
T Sunburst and Rose of Sharon—
from a quilt in Safford and Bishop,
pg. 193

12.93
T Double Tulip—
Webster, plate 30
Double Peony and Wild Rose—
Hall and Kretsinger, pg. 109

12.95
T Irish Beauty—
Mrs. Danner

12.97
T Oriental Poppy—
Kretsinger in Hall and Kretsinger

Four Fruits (& Miscellaneous)/Floral Center 13

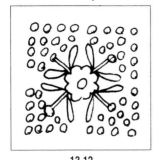

13.12
T Unnamed—
in *Modern Priscilla* 1925

13.13
T Foundation Rose and Pine
Tree—
Shelburne Museum

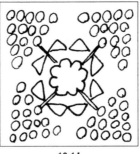

13.14
T Cherry—
Kimball

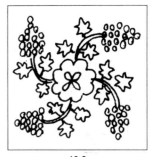

13.2
T Unnamed—
quilt in MacDowell/Michigan

13.31
T Watermelon—
Horton/*Social Fabric*, pg. 24

13.32
T Melon Patch—
Ickis, pg. 127

13.41
T Mrs. Harris's Colonial Rose—
Hall and Kretsinger, pg. 111

13.43
T Edith Hall's Rose—
Ramsey/Tennessee

13.52
T Unnamed—
from an album dated 1863

13.54
T Planet Jupiter—
Nancy Cabot, *Chicago Tribune* 1936

13.6
T Unnamed—
from an album dated 1853

13.7
T Unnamed—
from an album dated 1847

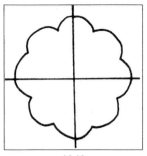

14.11
T Unnamed

14.12
Autograph—
from a quilt ca. 1935 in Arkansas
book

14.13
Unnamed—
Needlecraft 1940

14.14
T Unnamed—
from a quilt ca. 1850 in
Havig/Missouri

14.16
T Friendship—
Safford and Bishop, pg. 193

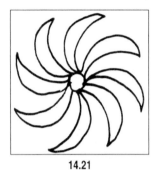

14.21
D Windblown Daisy—
Nancy Cabot, *Chicago Tribune* 1933

14.22
T Unnamed—
from an album dated 1850

14.23
T Zinnia—
Nancy Cabot, *Chicago Tribune* 1934

14.24
D Yellow Hemstitch—
Nancy Cabot, *Chicago Tribune*

14.25
D Blue Meadow Flower—
Nancy Cabot, *Chicago Tribune* 1937

14.26
D Double Dahlia Block—
Nancy Cabot, *Chicago Tribune* 1937

14.3
T Star Flower—
Nancy Cabot, *Chicago Tribune* 1933

14.41
T Snowflake—
Nancy Cabot, *Chicago Tribune* 1934

14.42
T Bouquet Quilt Block—
Comfort

14.52
D Tulip Wreath—
Nancy Cabot, *Chicago Tribune* 1933

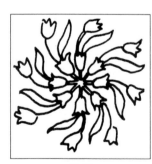

14.54
D Windblown Tulip—
Webster

14.57
T Unnamed—
from an album dated 1847

14.59
T Unnamed—
from an album dated 1863

14.61
T The Rose Bud—
Mrs. Danner, Books 1 & 2
Whig Rose—
Mrs. Danner, Books 1 & 2

14.62
T Whig Rose—
Aunt Martha, *Prize-Winning Quilts*

14.63
T Whig Rose—
Ramsey/Tennessee

14.64
T Whig Rose—
The Household ca. 1912
Rose Bud Wreath—
Ladies Art Company #498

14.65
T Mrs. Kretsinger's Rose—
Hall and Kretsinger, pg. 116

14.66
T Yellow Rose—
Nancy Cabot, *Chicago Tribune* 1933

14.67
T Whig Rose—
Peto, *American Quilts*

14.71
D Mimosa Wreath—
Nancy Cabot, *Chicago Tribune* 1936

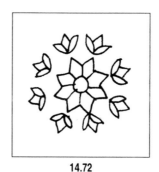

14.72
Ipswich Bouquet—
Nancy Cabot, *Chicago Tribune* 1938

14.73
T The Tulip Pattern—
Ladies Home Journal 1908

14.74
T Conventional Rose—
Hall and Kretsinger, pg. 109

14.75
T Rose of Tennessee—
Nancy Cabot, *Chicago Tribune* 1933

14.76
T Roses and Tulips—
Nancy Cabot, *Chicago Tribune* 1933

14.77
T Unnamed—
from an album dated 1846

14.78
T Unnamed—
from a quilt ca. 1850 in Spencer
Museum of Art

14.79
D Lavender Lace Flower—
Nancy Cabot, *Chicago Tribune* 1934

14.81
T Rose of Sharon—
Hall and Kretsinger, pg. 112

14.82
T Unnamed—
found in several mid-nineteenth
century quilts primarily from Garrard
County, Kentucky

14.83
T Eight Pointed Star with
Sprigs of Berries—
Sienkeiwicz

14.841
T Rose of Sharon—
from a quilt ca. 1850 in Kimball, pg.
146

14.843
T The Ladies' Dream—
Mrs. Danner

14.844
T Pumpkin Blossom—
Nancy Cabot, *Chicago Tribune*

14.847
T Unnamed—
from a quilt in Ramsey/Tennessee

14.848
T Pomegranate—
from a quilt ca. 1890 in
Uncoverings 1984

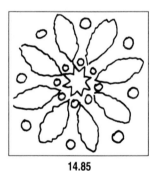

14.85
T Oak Leaf and Cherries—
from a quilt Texas Heritage Quilt
Society

14.87
T Unnamed—
from an album dated 1846

14.91
T Unnamed—
Farm and Fireside

14.93
T Unnamed—
from a quilt ca. 1850 in Safford and
Bishop, pg. 104

14.95
T Double Hearts—
from a quilt dated 1853 in Safford
and Bishop, pg. 193

14.97
T The United Hearts—
Capper's Weekly

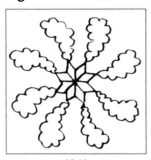

15.12
T Princess Feather—
Ladies Art Company #325
Star and Plumes—
Hall and Kretsinger

15.14
T Washington Feather—
Nancy Cabot, *Chicago Tribune* 1938

15.16
T Princess Feathers—
Safford and Bishop

15.18
T Princess Feather—
Finley

15.22
T Feather Rose—
Hall and Kretsinger

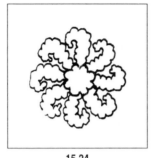

15.24
T Princess Feather—
Nancy Cabot, *Chicago Tribune* 1933

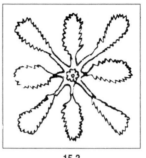

15.3
T Princess Feathers—
Webster

15.4
T Ben Hur's Chariot Wheel—
Hall and Kretsinger
Princess Feather—
Hall and Kretsinger

15.52
T Princess Feather with
Oak Leaves—
Holstein/Kentucky

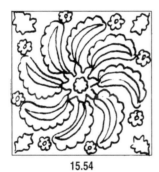

15.54
T Princess Feather—
from a quilt dated 1873 in Spencer
Museum of Art

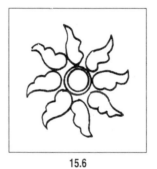

15.6
T Unnamed—
from an album dated 1846

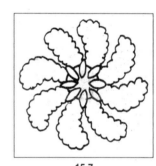

15.7
T Cucumber—
Roberson/North Carolina

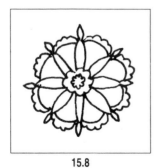

15.8
T Unnamed—
The Farmer's Wife October, 1929

15.91
T Snowflake—
from a quilt ca. 1860

15.93
T Unnamed—
from a quilt dated 1872 in
Roberson/North Carolina, pg. 90
Carolina Medallion—
Uncoverings 1987

15.98
T Unnamed—
from an album dated 1854

16.1
Hawthorne Berries—
Nancy Cabot, *Chicago Tribune* 1935

16.2
D Tangerine—
Nancy Cabot, *Chicago Tribune* 1936

16.3
T Grape and Morning Glory—
Carlie Sexton

16.4
D Honeysuckle—
Nancy Cabot, *Chicago Tribune* 1935

16.5
T Tree of Life—
People's Popular Monthly 1915

16.55
T Martha's Vineyard—
Mountain Mist #28

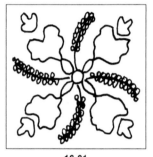

16.61
T Currants and Cockscombs—
Webster

16.62
T Coxcombs and Currants—
Nancy Cabot, *Chicago Tribune* 1935
Spray and Buds—
Nancy Cabot, *Chicago Tribune* 1935

16.63
T Cockscomb and Currants—
from a quilt ca. 1890 in
Ramsey/Tennessee

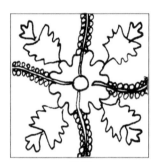

16.64
T Oak Leaf Variant—
from a quilt ca. 1860 in
Holstein/Kentucky, pg. 39

16.65
T Flowering Almond—
Comfort
Chestnut Berry—
Comfort February, 1926

16.66
T Poinsettia—
Finley, plate 73

16.67
T Grapes and Oak Leaf—
Roan/Goschenhoppen

16.68
T Cockscombs and Currants—
from a quilt ca 1870
Ramsey/Tennessee

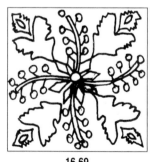

16.69
T Unnamed—
Lasansky, *In The Heart of
Pennsylvania* pg. 35

16.7
Tomato Flower—
Denver Art Museum

17.11

T Hickory Leaf—Ladies Art Company #70; Job's
Patience—*Country Life* February, 19; Orange
Peel—Carlie Sexton in *Country Gentleman* July, 1926;
The Reel—Finley; Compass—Carlie Sexton;
Order #11—McKim; Orange Slices—Shelburne
Museum; Oak Leaf—Beth Gutcheon. (See as a
pieced design #3110.)

17.12

T Irish Chain—
Hearth and Home

17.13

T Hickory Leaf—
Hearth and Home

17.14

T Unnamed—
from an album dated 1847

17.15

T Soul Knot—
Hearth and Home

17.16

T California Oak Leaf—
Ladies Art Company #497

17.17

T Bear Paw—
Mrs. Danner, ca. 1930
Oak Leaf and Reel—
Mrs. Danner, ca. 1970

17.18

T True Lover's Knot—
Carlie Sexton

17.19

T California Oak Leaf—
Needlecraft 1929

17.20

T Oak Leaf—
Ickis

17.21

T Hero's Crown—
Finley, pg. 124

17.22

T Fredonia Oak Leaf—
Mrs. Danner

17.23

T Crown of Oaks—
Nancy Cabot, *Chicago Tribune* 1937

17.24

T Oak Leaf—
possibly *Household Magazine*,
ca. 1920

17.25

T Oak Leaf and Acorn—
Hall and Kretsinger pg. 118

17.26

T Unnamed—
from a quilt ca. 1835 in the
Shelburne Museum

17.27
T Oak Leaf Pattern—
Country Life February, 1923

17.32
T Harrison Rose—
Ladies Art Company #187

17.33
T Nebraska Oak Leaf—
Wheeler/Brooks #5830

17.34
T Rose of Sharon—
Carlie Sexton

17.35
T Marigold—
Nancy Cabot, *Chicago Tribune* 1937
Rose in a Ring—
Aunt Martha, *Prize-Winning Quilts*
Ragged Robin—
Mrs. Danner

17.36
T Poppy—
Rural New Yorker

17.4
T Unnamed—
from a quilt ca. 1840

17.51
T Pineapple—
Horton/*Social Fabric*, pg. 38

17.52
T Prickly Pear—
Texas Heritage Quilt Society

17.53
T Unnamed—
Texas Heritage Quilt Society

17.6
T Sunburst—
from a quilt ca. 1892 in Davis

17.72
T Unnamed—
from an album dated 1845

17.73
T Oak Leaf Variation—
Safford and Bishop, pg. 162

17.81
Rose Point—
Nancy Cabot, *Chicago Tribune*

17.82
Aunt Flora's Bouquet—
Nancy Cabot, *Chicago Tribune* 1936

17.83
D Scotch Thistle—
Nancy Cabot, *Chicago Tribune* 1935

18.11
Cock's Comb—
Ickis pg. 72

18.13
Rose of the Wilderness—
Comfort

18.14
T Spiced Pinks—
Nancy Cabot, *Chicago Tribune* 1933
Pinks—
Nancy Cabot, *Chicago Tribune* 1938

18.22
T Combination Rose—
Carlie Sexton

18.24
T Democrat Rose—
The Household ca. 1912

18.32
T Unnamed—
Comfort February, 1926

18.33
T Spice Pink—
Finley, plate 64
Tea Rose—
Carlie Sexton

18.35
T The Whig Rose—Finley, plate 19
Democrat Rose—Hall and Kretsinger 114
Antique Rose—Mrs. Danner

18.37
T Tea Rose—
Nancy Cabot, *Chicago Tribune* 1935

18.4
T Rose Tree Block—
Carlie Sexton, *Old Fashioned
Quilts*, pg. 21

18.5
T Democratic Rose—
Nancy Cabot, *Chicago Tribune* 1936

18.6
T Tea Rose—
Nancy Cabot, *Chicago Tribune* 1933

18.72
T Running Rose—
Farm and Fireside September, 1929

18.74
T Antique Rose—Hall and Kretsinger
T Old Spice Pink—*Farm Journal* 1949
Similar block called Harvest
Rose—*Comfort*

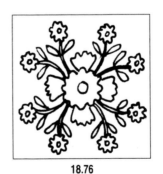

18.76
T Rose of Sharon—
Hall and Kretsinger, pg. 113

18.78
T Unnamed—
from a quilt in the *Quilt
Engagement Calendar*

Four plus Four Elements/Combs 18

18.79
T Whig Rose—
Bishop/Knopf, pg. 162

18.81
T California Rose—
Bishop/Knopf, pg. 164

18.83
T Rose of Sharon—
Holstein/Kentucky, pg. 70

18.85
T Unnamed—
Fox, *Small Endearments*, pg. 33

18.88
T Rose of Sharon Variation—
Horton, *Social Fabric*, pg. 22

18.92
T Whig Rose—
Ickis, pg. 134

18.94
T Unnamed—
Kansas Quilt Project #Ha140

18.96
T Unnamed—
Fox/Utah pg.24

Four Plus Four Elements 16–25

19.12
T Rose and Oak Leaf—
Ickis, pg. 5

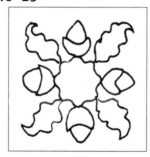

19.13
T Acorn and Oak Leaf—
Mountain Mist Oak
Leaves and Acorns—
Nancy Cabot, *Chicago Tribune* 1933

19.15
T Mahoning Rose—
Nancy Cabot, *Chicago Tribune* 1936

19.17
T Kentucky Rose—
Nancy Cabot, *Chicago Tribune* 1934

19.18
T The Oak Leaf—
Nancy Page (from the Leaf
series quilt)

19.19
T Oak Leaf and Acorn—
unknown clipping ca. 1890

19.22
T Oak Leaf—
from a quilt ca. 1860

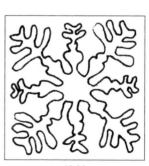

19.23
T Red Oak Block—
Nancy Cabot, *Chicago Tribune* 1937

19.24
T Forest—
from a quilt dated 1861 in the Art
Institute of Chicago

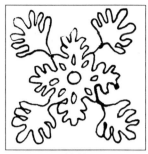

19.26
T Unnamed—
from an album dated 1844

19.31
T Unnamed—
from a quilt ca. 1850
Cochise County—
Ladies Circle Patchwork Quilts
(similar)

19.33
T Unnamed—
from a quilt in the *Quilt
Engagement Calendar* 1984,
plate 46

19.35
T Tulip Cross—
Woodard & Greenstein, plate 81
Princess Feather and Tulip—
Safford and Bishop pg. 193

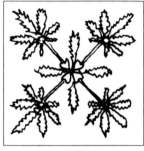

19.37
T Mountain Laurel—
Hall and Kretsinger, pg. 109

19.38
T Cockscomb—
Kimball

19.39
T Unnamed—
Lasansky, *Pieced by Mother*

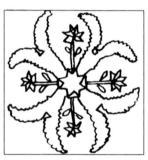

19.42
T Cactus—
Roan/Goschenhoppen

19.43
T Flowering Fan—
Quilt Engagement Calendar 1977,
plate 35

19.44
T Jester's Plume—
Quilter's Newsletter Magazine #177

19.46
T Star and Plume—
Finley, pg. 63

19.52
T Tulip Design—
Ickis, pg. 109

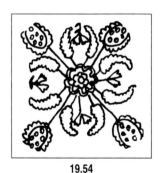

19.54
T The Rose and Thorn—
Quilter's Newsletter Magazine #191,
pg. 53

19.56
T Persian Block—
Nancy Cabot, *Chicago Tribune* 1937

19.58
T Conventional Applique—
Webster

19.62
T The Feather—
from a quilt ca. 1890 in
Uncoverings 1984

19.64
T Unnamed—
Safford and Bishop, pg. 194

19.72
T Unnamed—
Lasansky, *Pieced by Mother*, pg. 51
Poppy Applique—
Woodard and Greenstein, Crib
Quilts, pg. 54

19.74
T Unnamed—
Woodard and Greenstein, pg. 51

19.75
T Coxcomb—
Quilter's Newsletter Magazine #165,
pg. 24

19.83
T Cock's Comb—
Woodard and Greenstein, *Crib
Quilts*, plate 85

19.85
T Unnamed

19.9
T Oriental Poppy—
Hall and Kretsinger
Similar pattern named Pink Rose—
Comfort

20.12
T Rose of Sharon—
Nancy Cabot, *Chicago Tribune*

20.14
Mountain Laurel—
Nancy Cabot, *Chicago Tribune* 1935

20.18
D Oregon Daisy—
Nancy Cabot, *Chicago Tribune*

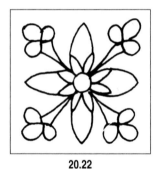

20.22
D Double Dahlia—
Nancy Cabot, *Chicago Tribune* 1938

20.24
D Full Blown Rose—
Nancy Cabot, *Chicago Tribune* 1937

20.26
T Clover Block—
Ladies Art Company #499

20.31
D California Poppy—
Nancy Cabot, *Chicago Tribune* 1934

20.32
D Cosmos—
Nancy Cabot, *Chicago Tribune* 1934

20.33

T Rose of Sharon—
Ickis, pg. 121

20.35

T Forest Bouquet—
Nancy Cabot, *Chicago Tribune* 1938

20.36

T Sadie's Choice—
Nancy Cabot, *Chicago Tribune* 1937

20.37

T Sadie's Choice—Carlie Sexton
Mexican Tea Rose—Nancy Cabot,
Chicago Tribune 1935
Balm of Gilead—Nancy Cabot,
Chicago Tribune
Peony—Hall and Kretsinger, pg. 111

20.38

T Full Blown Rose—
Nancy Cabot, *Chicago Tribune* 1933
June Rose—
Nancy Cabot, *Chicago Tribune* 1937

20.42

T Portulaca—
Nancy Cabot, *Chicago Tribune*

20.44

T Tulip—
from a quilt dated 1888,
Roberson/North Carolina, pg. 174

20.52

T Unnamed—
unknown clipping 1916

20.54

T Rose of Sharon—
Finley

20.62

Bachelor's Buttons—
Nancy Cabot, *Chicago Tribune* 1935

20.64

D Appliqued Lotus—
Nancy Cabot, *Chicago Tribune* 1936

20.66

T The Tulip—
Country Life February, 1923

20.68

T Rose of Sharon—
Source not found

20.69

T Unnamed

20.72

T Sharon Rose—
Rural New Yorker

20.8

D Flowered Cross—
Nancy Cabot, *Chicago Tribune* 1934
Five Roses—
Nancy Cabot, *Chicago Tribune* 1938

20.92
T Democrat Rose—
Source not found

20.94
T Rose of Sharon—
from a quilt ca. 1860, in *Kentucky Quilts*, pg. 37

20.96
D String of Beads—Aunt Martha
Studios Beads—Nancy Cabot,
Chicago Tribune 1933
Poinsettia—Aunt Martha

20.97
T Diamond Vine—
Nancy Cabot, *Chicago Tribune* 1936

20.98
D Lavender Puzzle—
Nancy Cabot, *Chicago Tribune* 1933

21.12
T Unnamed—
from an album dated 1852

21.13
T Poinsettia—
Webster (alternated with #33.13)

21.14
T Dogwood—
Rural New Yorker

21.22
T Laurel Leaves—
Safford and Bishop, pg. 158

21.24
T Pine Tree—
Needlecraft Magazine 1933

21.26
T Goldenrod—
Nancy Cabot, *Chicago Tribune* 1935

21.28
T Crossed Laurel Spray—
Sienkeiwicz

21.32
T Delphinium—
Nancy Cabot, *Chicago Tribune*

21.34
D Fuschia—
Nancy Cabot, *Chicago Tribune* 1937

21.36
T Horse Chestnut—
Nancy Cabot, *Chicago Tribune* 1935

21.38
D Appliqued Rose Petal—
Ickis, pg. 7

Four plus Four Elements 16–25

21.42
D Virginia Stock—
Nancy Cabot, *Chicago Tribune* 1934

21.44
D Clematis—
Nancy Cabot, *Chicago Tribune* 1934

21.46
T Mexican Rose—
Hall and Kretsinger, pg. 109

21.52
T Unnamed—
from an album dated 1859

21.54
T Tulip Quilt—
Modern Priscilla 1925
Tulip Cross—
Ladies Art Company #A261

21.56
T Holland Tulip—
Nancy Cabot, *Chicago Tribune* 1937

21.58
T Pennsylvania Tulip—
Country Home ca. 1935

21.62
D Peony—
Nancy Cabot, *Chicago Tribune* 1934

21.64
T Unnamed—
from an album dated 1855

21.66
D Swordbush—
Nancy Cabot, *Chicago Tribune* 1936

21.68
D Passion Flower—
Nancy Cabot, *Chicago Tribune*

21.72
Unnamed—
Modern Priscilla March, 1926
Hearts and Flowers—
Nancy Cabot, *Chicago Tribune* 1935

21.74
D Tulip Applique—
Wheeler/Brooks

21.82
Tulip Wreath—
Nancy Cabot, *Chicago Tribune* 1934
Tulip Circle—
Nancy Cabot, *Chicago Tribune*

21.84
Yellow Lily Block—
Nancy Cabot, *Chicago Tribune* 1936

21.86
Lilies of France—
Nancy Cabot, *Chicago Tribune* 1936

21.88

D Roses in the Snow—
Country Home ca. 1935

21.92

D March Tulip—
Sophie LaCroix

21.94

D Floral Wreath—
Grandma Dexter
Rio Wreath—
Nancy Cabot, *Chicago Tribune*

21.96

D Oriental Magnolias—
Nancy Cabot, *Chicago Tribune*

22.12

T Mexican Rose—
Nancy Cabot, *Chicago Tribune* 1933

22.13

T Mexican Rose—
McKim

22.15

T Mexican Rose—
Hall and Kretsinger, pg. 116

22.2

T Mrs. Brown's Peony—
Mrs. Danner

22.32

T Meadow Daisy—
Nancy Cabot, *Chicago Tribune* 1933

22.34

D Dogwood Block—
Nancy Cabot, *Chicago Tribune* 1935

22.41

T Mexican Rose—
Ladies Art Company #186
Aztec Rose—
Nancy Cabot, *Chicago Tribune* 1937

22.42

T Mexican Rose—
Webster, fig. 37

22.43

T Unnamed—
from an album dated 1855

22.44

T Meadow Daisy—
Finley, pg. 125
Black-Eyed Susan—
Hall and Kretsinger

22.45

T Forget Me Not—
Modern Priscilla, 917

22.47

T Unnamed—
from an album dated 1847

Four plus Four Elements 16–25

22.51
Tulip—
Comfort

22.52
D Sweet Peas—
Nancy Cabot, *Chicago Tribune* 1935

22.54
D Iris—
Capper's Weekly
Similar pattern called Bearded Iris—
Hinson/Quilting Manual

22.62
D Jonquils—
Nancy Cabot, *Chicago Tribune* 1934

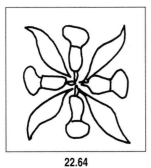

22.64
D Tassel Flower—
Nancy Cabot, *Chicago Tribune* 1934

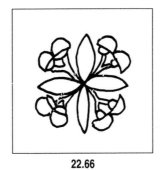

22.66
D Mexican Rosebud—
Nancy Cabot, *Chicago Tribune* 1934

22.72
T Coxcomb—
Shelburne Museum

22.74
D Cleome—
Nancy Cabot, *Chicago Tribune* 1934

22.83
D Four Lotus Blossoms—
Nancy Cabot, *Chicago Tribune* 1938

22.85
Easter Lilies—
Hall and Kretsinger, pg. 111

23.12
T Oak Leaf—
Finley, plate 20

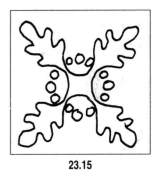

23.15
T Oak Leaf and Cherries—
Hall and Kretsinger, pg. 119

23.17
T Oak Leaf—
Needlecraft Magazine 1930

23.2
T Single Carnation—
Comfort

23.3
T Cockscomb—
Comfort
Lemon Lily—
Comfort

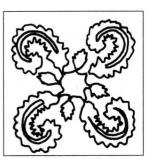

23.4
T Prince's Feather—
Comfort

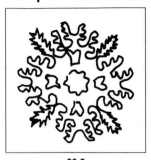

23.5
T Unnamed—
from an album dated 1848

23.6
T Unnamed—
from a quilt in the *Quilt Engagement Calendar* 1975, plate 26

23.7
T Unnamed—
from an album dated 1846

24.1
D Valentine—
Needlecraft Magazine 1933

24.2
T Unnamed—
from an album

24.3
D Virginia Stock—
Nancy Cabot, *Chicago Tribune* 1934

24.4
T Double Hearts—
Sienkeiwicz

24.5
T Hearts—
Art Insitute of Chicago

24.6
T Cactus Design—
St. Louis Fancy Work #1214

24.7
T Unnamed—
from a quilt in the *Quilt Engagement Calendar* 1991, plate 19

24.82
T Hearts and Diamonds—
Nancy Cabot, *Chicago Tribune* 1936

24.84
T Unnamed—
from an album dated 1865

24.86
T Hearts and Diamonds in Applique —
Kansas City Star 1944

25.12
T Trumpet Vine—
Sienkeiwicz, *Spoken Without a Word*

25.14
T Unnamed—
from an album dated 1850

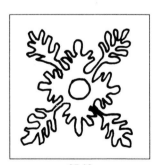

25.16
T Unnamed—
from an album dated 1852

25.18
T Unnamed—
from an album dated 1847

25.21
D Tulip Swirl—
Boag kit

25.22
North Carolina Rose—
Ickis, pg. 96

25.23
T The Lotus Flower—
Nancy Cabot, *Chicago Tribune*

25.24
D Four Tulips—
Nancy Cabot, *Chicago Tribune* 1935

25.26
T Conventional Tulips—
Webster

25.27
Garden of Light—
Nancy Cabot, *Chicago Tribune* 1938

25.3
D Farmer's Barometer—
Nancy Cabot, *Chicago Tribune* 1936

25.4
D Verbena—
Nancy Cabot, *Chicago Tribune* 1934

25.5
D Fringed Tulips—
Nancy Cabot, *Chicago Tribune* 1935

25.6
D Lilacs—
Nancy Cabot, *Chicago Tribune* 1935

25.7
D Leaves in the Wind—
Nancy Cabot, *Chicago Tribune* 1935

25.82
Spice Pinks—
Mrs. Danner 1934. See as a pieced
block #2527

25.84
Sweetheart Garden—
Nancy Cabot, *Chicago Tribune* 1933
See variations of this structure
classified as pieced designs
#2525—2528

25.86
Posies Around the Square—
Needlecraft Magazine 7/1934

25.9
T Grandmother's
Engagement Ring—
Mountain Mist. See #91 and as a
pieced pattern #2529

26.12
D Shamrock—
Kansas City Star 1932

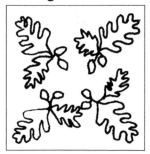

26.14
T Oak Leaf Wreath—
Ickis, pg. 54

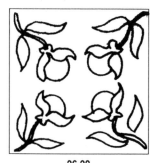

26.22
Rose of Lemoine—
Nancy Cabot, *Chicago Tribune*

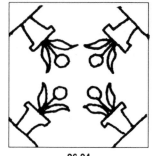

26.24
D Winter Garden—
Nancy Cabot, *Chicago Tribune* 1937

26.32
D Tulip Square—
Wilkinson

26.34
D Tulip—
Aunt Martha

26.36
D Tulip—
Webster design in *Ladies Home Journal* August, 1911

26.42
Rose Spray Square—
Wilkinson

26.44
T Wild Rose Design—
Wilkinson

26.45
D Wild Rose Design—
Modern Priscilla 1925

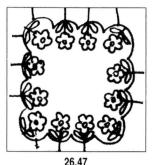

26.47
D Garden Paths—
Nancy Cabot, *Chicago Tribune* 1937

26.48
T Unnamed—
Lazansky, *Pieced by Mother*, plate 50

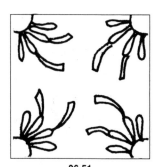

26.51
D Daisy Applique—
Hall and Kretsinger, pg. 104

26.52
D Daisy—
Carlie Sexton

26.53
D The Field Daisy—
Webster design in *Ladies Home Journal* August, 1911

26.62
D Pansies—
Nancy Cabot, *Chicago Tribune* 1938

26.63
D Poinsettia—
Grandmother Clark

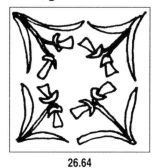

26.64
D Dancing Daffodil—
Mountain Mist

26.65
D Daffodils and Butterflies—
Webster design, *Ladies Home
Journal* August, 1911

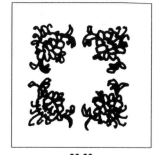

26.66
D Water Lilies—
Rainbow stamped block #465B

26.67
D Iris—
Webster design, *Ladies Home
Journal* August, 1911

26.68
D Iris—
Nancy Cabot, *Chicago Tribune* 1935

26.69
D Iris—
Webster design, *Ladies Home
Journal* August, 1911

26.72
D Unnamed—
Nancy Cabot, *Chicago Tribune*

26.73
D Sunshine—
Webster design, *Ladies Home
Journal* August, 1911

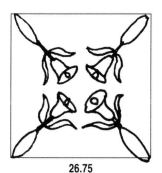

26.75
D Morning Glory Net—
Nancy Cabot, *Chicago Tribune* 1937

26.82
T Watermelon—
Horton/*Social Fabric*, pg. 24

26.84
Autograph Quilt—
from a quilt ca. 1925 in Arkansas
Quilters Guild

26.86
D Hearts and Flowers—
From a quilt dated 1937 in *North
Carolina Quilts*, pg. 77

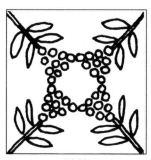

26.92
T Cherry—
Carlie Sexton

26.94
T Grapes and Vines—
Webster, fig. 66

26.96
T Unnamed—
from an album dated 1848

27.12

T Chrysthanthemum—Ladies Art Company
#408; Friendship Ring—McKim;
Aster—McKim; Grandmother's
Sunbonnet—*Prairie Farmer*; Grandmother's
Sunburst—*Wallace's Farmer* 10/12/1928 See
as a pieced pattern #3488

27.13

T Aster—
Meeker See as a pieced pattern
#3472

27.14

T Sunflower—
Home Art
Landon Sunflower—
Kansas City Star 9/12/1936 See as
a pieced pattern #3473

27.15

T China Aster—*Rural New Yorker* 1930
Aster—
Nancy Cabot, *Chicago Tribune* 1933
See as a pieced pattern #3474 and
#3485

27.22

T Unnamed—
from an album dated 1847

27.24

D Sunflower—
Nancy Cabot, *Chicago Tribune* 1933
Kansas Sunflower—
Nancy Cabot, *Chicago Tribune*
1938 See as a pieced pattern #3459

27.3

D Dresden Plate—
Mountain Mist See as a pieced
pattern #3489.5

27.4

D Sunflower—
Needlecraft Magazine 1931 See as
a pieced pattern #3492

27.5

D Love in the Mist—
Nancy Cabot, *Chicago Tribune* 1934

27.62

D Mountain Star—
Mountain Mist

27.64

D Sparkling Star—
Rainbow

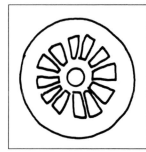

27.7

T Fortune's Wheel—
Hearth and Home

27.81

D Double Poppy—
Nancy Cabot, *Chicago Tribune*
See as a pieced pattern #3460

27.83

T Unnamed—
from an album dated 1855

27.85

D Kansas Sunflower—
Nancy Cabot, *Chicago Tribune* 1936

27.87

D Pinwheel Bouquet—
Nancy Cabot, *Chicago Tribune* 1935

28.12
T Tulip Block—
Ladies Art Company #65
Tulip—
Hearth and Home

28.13
T Dutch Tulip—
Nancy Cabot, *Chicago Tribune* 1935

28.15
T Single Tulip—
Hearth and Home

28.16
Tulip—
from a quilt dated 1932
in *North Carolina Quilts*

28.17
T Anna's Irish Tulip—
Hall and Kretsinger, pg. 122

28.18
T Colonial Tulip—
Hall and Kretsinger, pg. 122

28.19
T Tulip Applique—
McKim in *Kansas City Star* 1929

28.2
D Pride of the Garden—
Wheeler/Brooks

28.32
T Anna Bauersfeld's Tulip—
Hall and Kretsinger, pg. 122

28.33
T Tulip—
from a quilt ca. 1875
in *North Carolina Quilts*, pg. 68

28.34
T Tulip and Sun—
from a quilt ca. 1890
in *North Carolina Quilts*, pg 69

28.36
T Unnamed—
Aunt Martha, *Prize-Winning Quilts*

28.37
T Appliqued Tulip—
Wheeler/Brooks

28.42
T Tulip—
Nancy Cabot, *Chicago Tribune*

28.44
T Unnamed—
from an album dated 1860

28.53
Tiger Lily—
Farmer's Wife 1932 (alternated with
Irish Chain block)

28.54
D Tulip—
Sophie LaCroix

28.62
D Tulips—
Nancy Cabot, *Chicago Tribune* 1935

28.66
D Tulip Garden—
Farmer's Wife 1937

28.67
D Unnamed—
Needlecraft Magazine 1940

28.68
T Unnamed—
from an album dated 1865

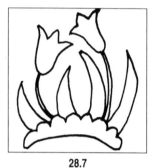

28.7
D Bell Flower—
Nancy Cabot, *Chicago Tribune* 1937

29.12
T Tulip—
from a quilt 1875–1900 in
North Carolina Quilts, pg. 66

29.14
T Tulip—
Nancy Cabot, *Chicago Tribune*

29.16
D Unnamed—
Aunt Martha

29.18
T Tulips—
source?

29.22
T Tulips—
Nancy Cabot, *Chicago Tribune*

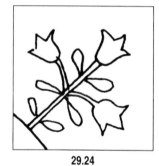

29.24
T Tiger Lily—
Hall and Kretsinger, pg. 118

29.25
T Mountain Lily—
Elizabeth Daingerfield,
"Patch Quilts and Philosphy"

29.26
Grandmother's Flower Quilt—
Nancy Cabot 1943

29.28
T Unnamed—
from an album dated 1852

29.33
T Single Tulip—
Webster, plate 35

29.35
T The Tulip Pattern—
Household Magazine

29.42
T Conventional Tulip—
Webster

29.43
T Regal Lily—
Ladies Art Company

29.44
T Rare Old Tulip—
Nancy Cabot, *Chicago Tribune* 1933

29.45
T June Lily—
Rural New Yorker

29.46
T Tiger Lily—
Finley, plate 37

29.47
T Original Tiger Lily—
Nancy Cabot, *Chicago Tribune* 1933

29.48
T Conventional Tulip—
Mountain Mist

29.49
T Rare Old Tulip—
Grandmother Clark Book 20, 1931

29.52
T Dutch Tulips—
from a quilt ca. 1890
in *Quilts of Tennessee*, pg. 1

29.53
T Tulip—
Aunt Martha

29.55
T Rare Old Tulip—
Comfort

29.62
T Tulip—
Wilkinson
Triple Tulip—
Hinson

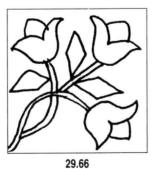

29.66
T Unnamed—
Aunt Martha, *Prize-Winning Quilts*

29.7
T Cotton Boll—
Art Institute of Chicago catalog

29.82
T Antique Tiger Lily—
Nancy Cabot, *Chicago Tribune* 1933

29.83
T Lily of the Valley—
Ladies Art Company #54

29.84
T Lily Quilt—
Nancy Cabot, *Chicago Tribune* 1938

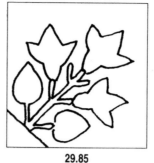

29.85
T White Day Lily—
Nancy Cabot *Chicago Tribune* 1935

29.86
T Potted Rose Bush—
Nancy Cabot, *Chicago Tribune* 1938

29.87
T Tiger Lily—
Nancy Cabot, *Chicago Tribune* 1933

29.89
T Conventional Tulip—
Country Home ca. 1935

29.91
T Tulip Plant—
Boag kit

29.92
T Tulip Design—
Farmer's Wife 10/1929

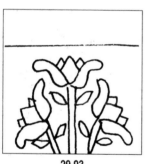

29.93
T Tulips—
Kansas City Star 1942
(rectangular block)

29.94
T Three Tulips—
Farm and Fireside September, 1929

29.95
D Tulip—
Carlie Sexton

29.962
T Tulips in Applique—
Comfort

29.964
T Early Tulips—
Nancy Cabot, *Chicago Tribune* 1937

29.97
D Tulip Pillow—
Wheeler/Brooks #7242

29.98
D Tulips in Applique—
Comfort

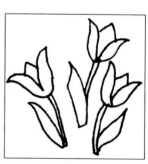

29.99
D Early Tulips—
Nancy Cabot, *Chicago Tribune* 1937

Bouquets 28–35/Tulips 28–30

30.12
T Unnamed—
from a repeat block quilt,
19th century

30.13
T Stylized Tulip—
Kimball, pg. 131

30.15
T Unnamed—
from an album dated 1847

30.17
D Tulip Designs—
St. Louis Fancy Work

Bouquets 28–35/Central Rose of Sharon 31

31.1
T Golden Rose of Virginia—
Nancy Cabot, *Chicago Tribune* 1933

31.23
T Pennsylvania Rose—
Capper's Weekly

31.25
T Harrison Rose—
Nancy Cabot, *Chicago Tribune* 1933
and Mountain Mist #L

31.26
T Harrison Rose—
Hall and Kretsinger, pg. 114

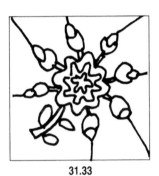

31.33
T Rose Applique—
McKim/*101 Quilt Patterns*, pg. 10

31.34
T Rappahannock Rose—
Nancy Cabot, *Chicago Tribune* 1937

31.42
T Rose of Sharon—
Webster

31.44
T Rose in Bud—
from a quilt ca. 1850 in Bacon,
pg 156 Much of this block is
actually pieced

31.46
T Rosebud Patchwork Quilt—
unknown clipping ca. 1890

31.52
T Rose of Sharon—
Hall and Kretsinger, pg. 112

31.54
T Virginia Rose—
Webster

31.6
T The Rose Sprig—
Carlie Sexton/*Old Fashioned Quilts*

Bouquets 28–35/Central Rose of Sharon 31

31.72
T Rose of Sharon—
Peto/*American Quilts*

31.73
T Rose of Sharon—
Nancy Cabot, *Chicago Tribune*

31.75
T Rose of Sharon—
McKim/*101 Quilt Patterns*, pg. 81

31.82
T Early Rose of Sharon—
Finley, plate 65

31.83
T Rose of Sharon—
Hall and Kretsinger, pg. 113

31.85
T Ohio Beauty—
quilt by Whitehill in Denver Art
Museum

31.87
T Unnamed—
from a quilt in Bishop and Coblentz,
pg. 100

31.92
T Unnamed—
from a quilt in Safford and Bishop,
pg. 184
Asymmetrical Rose—
Kimball

31.93
T American Beauty Rose—
Webster in *Ladies Home Journal*,
1911 See similar patterns
numbered 45.23

31.95
T Unnamed—
from a quilt dated 1855 in
Lasansky/*Pieced By Mother*, pg. 67

31.97
T Unnamed—
from a quilt dated 1855 in
Lasansky/*Pieced By Mother*, pg. 67

31.99
T Unknown—
from a quilt in Roberson/North
Carolina, pg. 95 The North Carolina
Project found several examples.

Bouquets/Miscellaneous 32–33

32.11
D Dogwood—
Wheeler/Brooks

32.12
D Meadow Rose—
Nancy Cabot, *Chicago Tribune* 1936

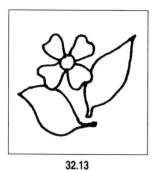

32.13
D Dogwood—
Nancy Cabot, *Chicago Tribune* 1936

32.14
D Wild Rose—
Aunt Martha/*Prize-Winning Quilts*
Aunt Martha's Wild Rose—
Hall and Kretsinger, pg. 111

32.22
D Bowknot—
Needlecraft Magazine 1935

32.24
D Unnamed—
Needlecraft Magazine 1940

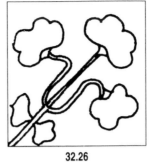

32.26
T Yellow Wildfire—
Nancy Cabot, *Chicago Tribune* 1938

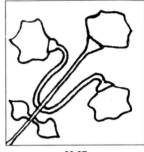

32.27
T Peony—
Elizabeth Daingerfield,
Ladies Home Journal 1912

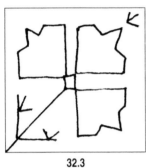

32.3
D Rose Geranium—
Nancy Cabot, *Chicago Tribune* 1935

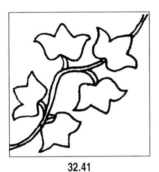

32.41
D Ivy—
Nancy Cabot, *Chicago Tribune* 1937

32.42
D Sage Brush Block—
Nancy Cabot, *Chicago Tribune* 1935

32.51
D Unnamed—
Successful Farming 6/1930

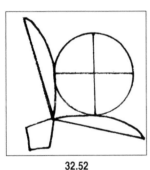

32.52
D Evening Flower Block—
Nancy Cabot, *Chicago Tribune* 1934

32.54
D Baby Chrysthanthemum—
Nancy Cabot, *Chicago Tribune* 1934

32.57
D Globe Thistle—
Nancy Cabot, *Chicago Tribune* 1934

32.58
D Marigolds—
Nancy Cabot, *Chicago Tribune* 1938

32.59
D Pompon—
Nancy Cabot, *Chicago Tribune* 1936

32.61
D Calla Lily—
Nancy Cabot, *Chicago Tribune* 1934

32.62
D Bluebells and Splendors—
Rainbow stamped block #720B

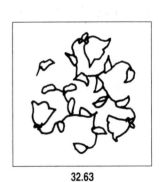

32.63
D Woodland Bells—
Rainbow stamped block #575c

32.71
T Unnamed—
from an album dated 1861

32.74
D Decorative Flowers—
Nancy Cabot, *Chicago Tribune* 1935

32.75
D Bluebell Quilt—
Wheeler/Brooks

32.76
D Lily of the Valley—
Wheeler/Brooks #1017

32.81
D Blue Bells—
Nancy Cabot, *Chicago Tribune* 1934

32.82
D Cathedral Bells—
Nancy Cabot, *Chicago Tribune* 1934

32.83
D Lilies of the Valley—
Nancy Cabot, *Chicago Tribune* 1935

32.84
D Bell and Flower—
Nancy Cabot, *Chicago Tribune* 1935

32.85
D Lily of the Valley—
Nancy Cabot, *Chicago Tribune*

32.87
D Wisteria—
Nancy Cabot, *Chicago Tribune* 1935

32.91
D Tree of Life—
Aunt Martha ca. 1933

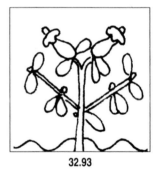

32.93
D Desert Bell Flower—
Nancy Cabot, *Chicago Tribune* 1936

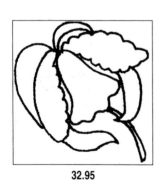

32.95
D Orchids—
Nancy Cabot, *Chicago Tribune* 1933

33.12
T The Love Rose—
Ladies Art Company #188

33.13
T Poinsettia—
Webster (alternated with #21.13)

33.15
T Cactus Flower—
Needlecraft Magazine 1935
Blooming Cactus—
Nancy Cabot, *Chicago Tribune* 1935

33.16
T Single Bud—
Nancy Cabot, *Chicago Tribune* 1938

33.18
T Heirloom Historic Quilt—
Wheeler/Brooks

33.21
T Whig Rose—
Webster, fig. 48

33.22
T Tiger Lily and Bud—
Nancy Cabot, *Chicago Tribune* 1935

33.24
T Whig Rose—
Hall and Kretsinger, pg. 114

33.25
T Lotus Flower—
Shelburne Museum

33.32
T Dixie Rose—
from a quilt ca. 1850
in *North Carolina Quilts*, pg.182

33.37
T Olive Branch—
Ladies Art Company #110
Tulip Design—
Wilkinson

33.41
D Unnamed—
Aunt Martha ca. 1933
Wild Flower—
Nancy Cabot, *Chicago Tribune* 1937

33.42
Old Dutch Tulip—
Hall and Kretsinger, pg. 122

33.43
D Canada Lily—
Nancy Cabot, *Chicago Tribune* 1933

33.44
D Rose Garden—
Nancy Cabot, *Chicago Tribune*

33.45
D Old Persia—
Nancy Cabot, *Chicago Tribune* 1937

33.46
D Flower Tree—
Grandmother Clark

33.47
D Flower Spears—
Nancy Cabot, *Chicago Tribune* 1936

33.48
D Fuschia Quilt—
Modern Priscilla 1925

33.52
D Poinsettia—
Webster design 1917

33.54
D Autumn Flowers—
Hall and Kretsinger, pg. 106

33.56
D Hollyhock—
Capper's Weekly

33.59
D Field Flowers—
Paragon

33.61
T Unnamed—
from a sampler dated 1855
in *North Carolina Quilts*

33.62
T Chrysthanthemum—
Arkansas Quilters Guild

33.63
D Chrysthanthemum—
Hearth and Home

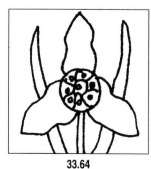

33.64
D Mexican Shell Flower—
Nancy Cabot, *Chicago Tribune* 1934

33.72
D Salvia—
Nancy Cabot, *Chicago Tribune* 1934

33.74
D Mignonette—
Nancy Cabot, *Chicago Tribune* 1934

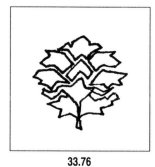

33.76
D Modern Flower Block—
Nancy Cabot, *Chicago Tribune* 1936

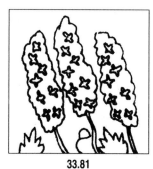

33.81
D Delphiniums—
Nancy Cabot, *Chicago Tribune*

33.83
D Cliveden Quilt—
McCall's

33.85
D Wayside Roses—
Webster ca. 1925

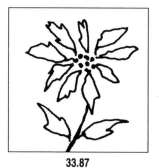

33.87
D Poinsettia—
Rainbow stamped block #841

33.9
T Shaw Family Pattern—
Whitehill in Denver Art Museum

Bouquets/Five Elements or Five-Lobed Flowers 34 & 35

34.11
D Burning Bush—
Nancy Cabot, *Chicago Tribune* 1934

34.12
D Viscaria—
Nancy Cabot, *Chicago Tribune* 1934

34.14
D Pansy Block—
Nancy Cabot, *Chicago Tribune*

34.16
D Columbine—
Nancy Cabot, *Chicago Tribune*

34.18
D Anemone—
Nancy Cabot, *Chicago Tribune* 1934

34.19
D Rose of the Field—
Needlecraft Magazine 1933

34.22
D Kentucky Columbine—
Nancy Cabot, *Chicago Tribune* 1936

34.24
D Larkspur—
Nancy Cabot, *Chicago Tribune*

34.26
D Rose of Heaven—
Nancy Cabot, *Chicago Tribune*

34.28
D Azalea—
Nancy Cabot, *Chicago Tribune* 1937

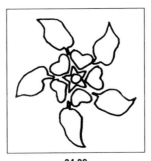

34.29
D Damask Rose—
Comfort

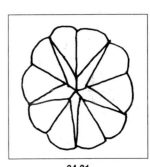

34.31
D Moonflower—
Nancy Cabot, *Chicago Tribune*

34.33
Texas Republic—
Nancy Cabot, *Chicago Tribune* 1936

34.42
D Corsage Bouquet—
Aunt Martha/*Prize-winning Quilts*
Morning Glory—
Hetty Winthrop (aka Nancy Cabot)

34.46
T Wild Rose Spray—
Nancy Cabot, *Chicago Tribune*
Spray with Wild Roses—
Nancy Cabot, *Chicago Tribune* 1945

34.47
T Wild Rose—
Carlie Sexton

34.48
T Modern Wild Rose—
Comfort

34.52
D Angel's Breath—
Nancy Cabot, *Chicago Tribune* 1934

34.54
D Wild Rose—
Ladies Art Company #447

34.56
D Jasmine—
Nancy Cabot, *Chicago Tribune* 1937

34.57
D Forget Me Not—
Nancy Cabot, *Chicago Tribune* 1938

34.58
D Unnamed—
Needlework Magazine 1923

34.59
D Snow in July—
Nancy Cabot, *Chicago Tribune* 1934

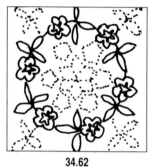

34.62
D Strawberry Block—
Nancy Cabot, *Chicago Tribune* 1938

34.64
D Wild Rose #3—
Nancy Cabot, *Chicago Tribune* 1933

34.65
D Wild Rose—
Nancy Cabot, *Chicago Tribune* 1933

34.67
D Verbena—
Rainbow stamped block

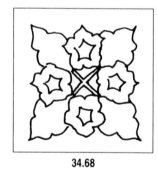

34.68
D Primrose—
Nancy Cabot, *Chicago Tribune*
Giant Primrose—
Nancy Cabot, *Chicago Tribune* 1938

34.69
D Morning Glory—
Ladies Art Company #418, also
Mountain Mist

34.72
D Wild Rose—
Comfort

34.74
D Wildwood Wreath—
Farmer's Wife

34.75
D Dogwood Flower—
Rainbow stamped block #177c

35.12
D Forget Me Not—
Mountain Mist #61

35.13
D Unnamed—
Needlecraft Magazine 1923

35.14
D Rose Spray—
Nancy Cabot, *Chicago Tribune* 1934

35.16
D Blue Petunia—
Nancy Cabot, *Chicago Tribune* 1938

35.17
D Rose Garden—
Nancy Cabot, *Chicago Tribune*

35.22
D Lily Applique—
Wheeler/Brooks #1721

35.23
D Golden Lily—
Nancy Cabot, *Chicago Tribune* 1933

35.24
D Cardinal Climber—
Nancy Cabot, *Chicago Tribune* 1934

35.25
D Hibiscus—
Nancy Cabot, *Chicago Tribune* 1933

35.27
D Hibiscus—
Nancy Cabot, *Chicago Tribune* 1934

35.31
D Flower Spray—
Nancy Cabot, *Chicago Tribune* 1935

35.33
D Baby Rose—
Nancy Cabot, *Chicago Tribune* 1933

35.34
D Unnamed—
Rainbow stamped block #315

35.35
D Super Gorgeous Apple
Blossom—
Rainbow stamped block #930

35.36
D Wild Rose of the Andes—
Rainbow stamped block #736e

35.37
D Wild Rose—
Nancy Cabot, *Chicago Tribune*

Bouquets/Five Elements or Five-Lobed Flowers 34 & 35

35.41
D Blue Trumpet Flower—
Nancy Cabot, *Chicago Tribune* 1937

35.43
D Wild Rose Bouquet—
Nancy Cabot, *Chicago Tribune*

35.44
D Scattered Morning Glories—
McCall's Needlework Winter,
1941–42

35.45
D Wisconsin Rose—
Nancy Cabot, *Chicago Tribune* 1933

35.46
D Hollyhock—
Wheeler/Brooks #403

35.47
D Source not found

35.49
D Marvel of Peru—
Rainbow stamped block #755d

35.5
D Irish Shamrock—
Rainbow stamped block #850d

35.6
D Prairie Pinks—
Nancy Cabot, *Chicago Tribune*

35.7
D Petunias—
Rainbow stamped block #854d

35.8
D Boutonnier—
Nancy Cabot, *Chicago Tribune* 1935

35.9
D Unnamed—
Rainbow stamped block #458

Six Petals or Six Elements 36

36.11
A Dainty Block—
Ladies Home Journal 1896

36.12
D Willow Squares—
Nancy Cabot, *Chicago Tribune* 1936

36.14
D Narcissus—
Nancy Cabot, *Chicago Tribune* 1936

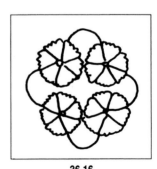

36.16
D Nasturtium—
Nancy Cabot, *Chicago Tribune* 1935

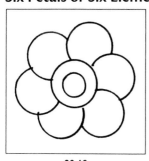

36.18
D Priscilla Alden—
Nancy Cabot, *Chicago Tribune* 1934

36.22
Tulip Wheel—
Marston and Cunningham

36.24
T Unnamed—
Aunt Martha/*Prize-winning Quilts*

36.25
T Emporia Rose—
Comfort

36.26
D Berkshire Beauty—
Nancy Cabot, *Chicago Tribune* 1937

36.32
Pennsylvania Good Luck Block—
Peto/*American Quilts*

36.33
T Mexican Rose—
Nancy Cabot, *Chicago Tribune* 1936

36.35
T Wild Rose—
Hall and Kretsinger, pg. 116

36.38
T Geometrical Rose—
Shelburne

36.43
D Solar System—
Nancy Cabot, *Chicago Tribune*

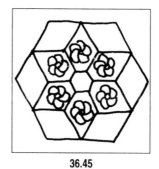

36.45
D Solomon's Garden—
Nancy Cabot, *Chicago Tribune*

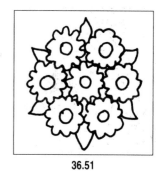

36.51
D Zinnia Bouquet—
Nancy Cabot, *Chicago Tribune* 1934

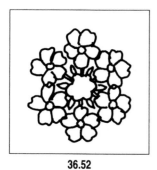

36.52
D Wreath of Violets—
Nancy Cabot, *Chicago Tribune* 1934
Violet Wreath—
Nancy Cabot, *Chicago Tribune* 1937

36.53
D Sweet William—
Nancy Cabot, *Chicago Tribune* 1934

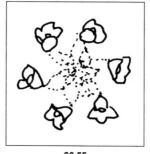

36.55
D Circle of Godetias—
Rainbow stamped block

36.56
T Cupid's Block—
Ladies Art Company #500

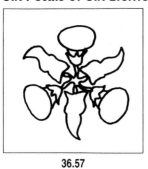

36.57
D Morning Glory—
Nancy Cabot, *Chicago Tribune* 1935

36.58
D Dianthus—
Nancy Cabot, *Chicago Tribune* 1934

36.59
D Cornflower—
Rainbow stamped block #830

36.61
D Snowflake—
Ladies Art Company #495
Snow Crystals—
Nancy Cabot, *Chicago Tribune*

36.62
D Snowflake--
Wheeler/Brooks #7236

36.63
D Christmas Rose—
Farm Journal 1938

36.65
D Snowflake—
Ladies Home Journal 1911

36.69
D Star and Epaulettes—
Nancy Cabot, *Chicago Tribune* 1936

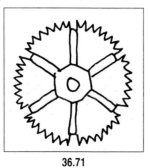

36.71
T Samoan Poppy—
Nancy Cabot, *Chicago Tribune* 1935

36.72
T October Foliage—
Nancy Cabot, *Chicago Tribune* 1936

36.73
T Esther's Plume—
Mrs. Danner
Indian Princess Feather—
Mrs. Danner

36.74
T Princess Feather—
Safford and Bishop, fig. 286

36.75
T Feather Rose—
Mrs. Danner

36.76
T California Plume—
Hall and Kretsinger, pg. 202

36.77
T Princess Feather—
Aunt Martha ca. 1933

36.81
D Old Fashioned Bouquet—
Nancy Cabot, *Chicago Tribune* 1934

Six Petals or Six Elements 36

36.82
T French Rose—
Aunt Martha

36.83
T Moss Ross—
Nancy Cabot, *Chicago Tribune* 1937

36.84
T Rose of Sharon—
Ladies Art Company #6056

36.85
D Wind Blown Rose—
Hall and Kretsinger, pg. 109

36.86
T Tallula Rose—
Nancy Cabot, *Chicago Tribune* 1937

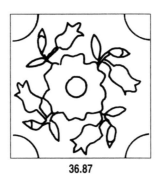

36.87
D Petunia and Bluebell—
Nancy Cabot, *Chicago Tribune*
Bluebells and Petunia—
Nancy Cabot, *Chicago Tribune*

36.88
D Unnamed—
McCall's

36.89
T Meadow Rose—
Nancy Cabot, *Chicago Tribune* 1936

Seven Petals

36.92
D Snowdrop Quilt—
St. Louis Fancy Work

36.94
D Snowdrop Quilt—
St. Louis Fancy Work
(these two alternate)

36.97
D Rose and Sunflowers—
Nancy Cabot, *Chicago Tribune* 1934

Bouquets/ Stars and Roses 37.1–37.2

37.11
T Maple Leaf—
Farmer's Wife 1932

37.12
T Double Tulip—
The Family 1913 (see variations of
these triple stars filed as pieced
designs #767-774)

37.13
T Tree of Life—
Comfort

37.14
T North Carolina Lily—
from a quilt ca. 1845

37.15
T Unnamed—
Modern Priscilla 3/1926

37.17
T Red Peony—
Nancy Cabot, *Chicago Tribune* 1933
Flowering Balsam—
Nancy Cabot, *Chicago Tribune* 1938

37.211
D Dahlia—
Ladies Art Company #6005

37.212
T Peonies—
Hall and Kretsinger, pg. 111

37.213
T Kentucky Peony—
Nancy Cabot, *Chicago Tribune* 1933

37.214
T Rose of Sharon—
from a quilt ca. 1880 in
Ramsey/*Tennessee*, pg. 42

37.215
T Original Rose—
Webster, plate 51

37.224
T Rose of Sharon—
Hall and Kretsinger, pg. 111

37.226
T Rose Tree—
McKim

37.232
D Rose and Primrose—
Nancy Cabot, *Chicago Tribune* 1934
Rose and Daisy—
Nancy Cabot, *Chicago Tribune* 1934

37.234
T Unnamed—
from an album dated 1854

37.236
T Unnamed—
from an album dated 1861

37.238
T Unnamed—
from an album dated 1861

37.144
T Unnamed—
from an album dated 1859

37.246
D Rose Tree—
from the border of a quilt designed
by Mountain Mist

37.25
T Unnamed—
this rose is typical of many
elaborate blocks in Baltimore
Album quilts

37.261
D Super Gorgeous
American Rose—
Rainbow stamped block #91

Bouquets/Stars and Roses 37.1–37.2

37.262
D Rose Petals—
Nancy Cabot, *Chicago Tribune*

37.263
D Unnamed—
Needlecraft Magazine 1929

37.264
D Rose Beauty—
Nancy Cabot, *Chicago Tribune* 1933

37.27
T Old Fashioned Flower Garden—
Hall and Kretsinger, pg. 106

37.28
D Rose Spray—
Comfort

37.293
T Moss Rose—
Hall and Kretsinger, pg. 170

37.294
T Four Square Rose—
MacDowell, Michigan Quilts, pg. 24

37.298
T Unnamed—
from a quilt ca. 1850
Prudence Penny

Bouquets/Water Lilies

37.3

37.31
D Magnolia Applique—
Wheeler/Brooks

37.311
D Water Lilies—
Mountain Mist

37.313
D Lotus Blossom—
Nancy Cabot, *Chicago Tribune* 1933

37.32
D Water Lilies—
Grandmother Clark

37.33
D Water Lily—
Nancy Cabot, *Chicago Tribune* 1934

37.34
D Lily Pond—
Ladies Art Company #4020
Water Lily—
Hall and Kretsinger

37.35
D Flower of Spring—
Kansas City Star 1936
(see pieced #799)

37.36
D Lily Design—
Comfort

Bouquets/Waterlillies 37.3

37.372
D Water Lily—
Rainbow stamped block #718c

37.373
D Water Lily—
Rainbow stamped block #718c

37.38
D Water Lily Circle—
Rainbow stamped block #800

37.39
D Unnamed—
Rainbow stamped block #727

Bouquets/Morning Flories 37.4

37.42
D Morning Glory—
Nancy Cabot, *Chicago Tribune* 1934
Giant Morning Glory—
Nancy Cabot, *Chicago Tribune* 1937

37.43
D Morning Glory—
Wheeler/Brooks

37.46
D Morning Glory—
St. Louis Fancy Work

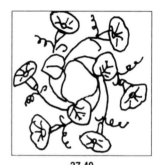

37.49
D Morning Glories in a Circle—
Rainbow stamped block #805

Bouquets/Poppies 37.5

37.51
D Poppy Applique—
Wheeler/Brooks

37.52
D Flanders Poppy—
Nancy Cabot, *Chicago Tribune* 1934

37.544
D Poppy Field—
Aunt Martha
(alternates with a Red Cross)

37.546
D Poppy Garden—
Nancy Cabot, *Chicago Tribune* 1933
(alternates with #37.548)

37.548
D Poppy Garden—
Nancy Cabot, *Chicago Tribune* 1933
(alternates with #37.546)

37.551
D Poppies—
Nancy Cabot, *Chicago Tribune* 1933

37.553
D Red Poppies—
Nancy Cabot, *Chicago Tribune*

37.555
D Poppy—
St. Louis Fancy Work

Bouquets/Poppies 37.5

37.56
D Poppies—
Rainbow stamped block #710

37.57
D Priscilla's Poppies—
Nancy Cabot, *Chicago Tribune* 1935

37.58
D Poppies—
Rainbow stamped block #320

37.59
D Field Flowers—
Nancy Cabot, *Chicago Tribune* 1934

Bouquets/Pansies 37.6

37.61
D Pansy—
Sears 1934

37.62
D Pansy Applique—
Wheeler/Brooks

37.63
D Pansy—
Star and Pansy Design—
Ladies Art Company

37.64
D Pansy—
Wheeler/Brooks

37.65
D Gay Print Pansy—
Needlecraft Magazine

37.662
D Pansies—
Rainbow stamped block #535s

37.664
D Gorgeous Pansies—
Rainbow stamped block #838

37.665
D Pansies—
Rainbow stamped block #300

Bouquets/Iris 37.7

37.67
D Pansies—
Wheeler/Brooks #7044

37.68
D Pansy Block—
Nancy Cabot, *Chicago Tribune* 1933

37.69
D Pansy Design—
Ladies Art Company #6065

37.7
D Flags—
Rainbow stamped block #712

Bouquets/Iris 37.7

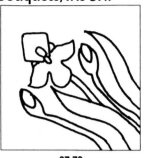

37.72
D Iris Applique—
McKim #369

37.73
D Unnamed—
Aunt Martha

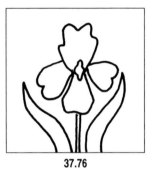

37.742
D Iris—
Mountain Mist

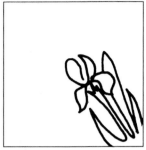

37.743
D Iris—
Boag kit

37.75
D Iris—
Ladies Art Company #6085

37.76
D Purple Iris—
Nancy Cabot, *Chicago Tribune* 1934

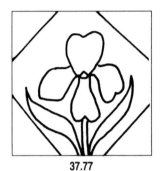

37.77
D Simple Iris—
Nancy Cabot, *Chicago Tribune* 1935

37.78
D Conventional Fleur-de-Lis—
Comfort
Tiger Lily—
Comfort

Bouquets/Daffodils 37.8

37.79
Iris—
Nancy Cabot, *Chicago Tribune* 1933

37.81
D Narcissus—
Wheeler/Brooks

37.82
D Daffodils—
Nancy Cabot, *Chicago Tribune*

37.84
D Daffodils—
Aunt Martha

37.85
D Jonquils—
Nancy Cabot, *Chicago Tribune* 1936

37.87
D Narcissus—
Nancy Cabot, *Chicago Tribune* 1933

37.88
D Rainbow Quilt—
Webster

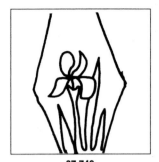

37.89
D Dancing Daffodil—
Home Art

37.913
D Conventional Flower—
Hearth and Home

37.915
D Friendship Dahlia—
Hall and Kretsinger, pg. 104

37.917
D Kansas Sunflower—
Capper's Weekly 1930

37.923
D Poinsettia—
Hall and Kretsinger, pg. 106

37.924
D Modern Poinsettia—
Nancy Cabot, *Chicago Tribune*

37.926
D Brown-Eyed Susans—
Nancy Cabot, *Chicago Tribune* 1933

37.932
Sunflower—
Nancy Cabot, *Chicago Tribune* 1936

37.934
T Old Sunflower—
Nancy Cabot, *Chicago Tribune* 1937

37.936
T Southern Sunflower—
Hearth and Home

37.94
T Unnamed—
from a quilt 1860–1885
Spencer Museum of Art

37.95
T Unnamed—
from a mid-nineteenth century quilt
in the *Quilt Engagement Calendar*
1979, pg. 23

37.96
Zinnia Border—
Mountain Mist

37.97
T Sunflower—
from a quilt ca. 1861 Vermont

37.981
D Blanket Flower—
Nancy Cabot, *Chicago Tribune* 1934

37.982
D Sun God—
Nancy Cabot, *Chicago Tribune*

37.99
D Feather Flower—
Nancy Cabot, *Chicago Tribune* 1934

38.1
T Unnamed—
from an album dated 1848

38.22
D Horn of Plenty—
Ladies Art Company

38.23
D Horn of Plenty—
Needlecraft Magazine

38.24
D Horn of Penty—
Nancy Cabot, *Chicago Tribune* 1933

38.25
D Ladies Art Company #6082

38.32
D Horn of Plenty—
Nancy Cabot, *Chicago Tribune*

38.34
D Horn of Plenty—
Paragon kit
Garden Bounty—
Wheeler/Brooks #662

38.4
D Horn of Plenty—
Hall and Kretsinger

38.52
T Unnamed—
from an album dated 1848. These
striped cornucopia are typical of
Baltimore Album quilts

38.54
T Unnamed—
from an album dated 1847

38.55
T Unnamed—
from an album dated 1840 (this
date seems a few years too early)

38.6
T Unnamed—
from a cut-out chintz quilt ca. 1830
in the Shelburne Museum #29

38.72
T Unnamed—
from an album dated 1861

38.76
T Unnamed—
from an album dated 1861

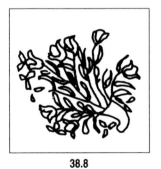

38.8
T Unnamed—
from a quilt dated 1814 in the
Shelburne Museum #140

38.9
T Unnamed—
from an album dated 1860

39.13

D A Charming Nosegay—
McKim
Old Fashioned Nosegay—
Hall and Kretsinger, pg. 106

39.15

D Nosegay—
Needlecraft Magazine 1933

39.24

D English Flower Garden—McKim
English Garden—*Capper's Weekly*
Old English Flower Garden—
Kansas City Star

39.25

D Dutch Roses—
Nancy Cabot, *Chicago Tribune* 1935

39.34

D Geranium—
Aunt Martha

39.36

D Magyar Flower Pot—
Nancy Cabot, *Chicago Tribune*

39.43

D Rose Flower Pot—
Mrs. Danner

39.45

D Pot of Tulips—
Nancy Cabot, *Chicago Tribune* 1933

39.46

D Unnamed—
Needlecraft Magazine 5/1923

39.48

D Tulip in a Pot—
Carlie Sexton
Cut Tulips—
Nancy Cabot, *Chicago Tribune* 1934

39.51

D Petunia—
Nancy Cabot, *Chicago Tribune* 1934

39.52

D Pot of Flowers—
Grandmother Clark Book 21, 1931

39.53

D Pot of Flowers—
Nancy Cabot, *Chicago Tribune* 1935

39.55

D Grandmother's Prize Quilt—
Wheeler/Brooks

39.57

D Sweetheart Rose—
Needlecraft Magazine

39.59

D Dahlia Flower Pot—
Nancy Cabot, *Chicago Tribune* 1937

39.6
D Phillipsburg (PA) Flower Pot—
Nancy Cabot, *Chicago Tribune* 1936

39.7
D Daffodil—
Herschnner (see as a series)

39.8
D Bluebell Block—
Nancy Cabot, *Chicago Tribune* 1936

39.9
D Gingham Bush—
Nancy Cabot, *Chicago Tribune* 1935

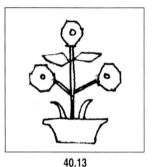

40.13
D Flowers in a Pot—
Ickis pg. 44

40.15
D Pot of Poppies—
Nancy Cabot, *Chicago Tribune*

40.22
D Box of Tulips—
Kansas City Star 3/7/1951

40.24
T Tulip Pot—
Marston and Cunningham

40.32
T Unnamed—
Modern Priscilla

40.35
D Yellow Iris—
Nancy Cabot, *Chicago Tribune* 1934

40.36
D Box of Pansies—
Nancy Cabot, *Chicago Tribune* 1933

40.38
D Unnamed—
Needlecraft Magazine 1923

40.41
T Sahara Rose—
Nancy Cabot, *Chicago Tribune* 1936

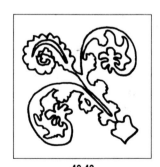

40.42
T Unnamed—
Webster, fig. 35

40.45
D Unnamed—
Successful Farming 6/1930

40.47
T Unnamed—
from an album dated 1865

40.5
Flower Urn—
Aunt Martha/*Prize-winning Quilts*

40.63
T Tulip—
Source not found

40.64
D Unnamed—
Aunt Martha/*Prize-winning Quilts*

40.66
D Unnamed—
Aunt Martha/*Prize-winning Quilts*

40.7
D Tulip Bowl—
Mountain Mist

40.9
D Source not found

41.12
T Coxcomb—
Nancy Cabot, *Chicago Tribune*

41.13
D Basket of Spring—
Rainbow
Flower of Spring—
Needlecraft Magazine 1923

41.16
T Flower Basket—
Hall and Kretsinger, pg. 186

41.19
T Lotus Blossom—
Bresenhan/Texas

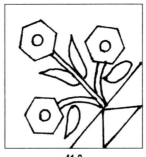

41.2
D Tile Flower—
Aunt Martha ca. 1933

41.3
T Seth Thomas Rose—
Kansas City Star 1929

41.42
T Coxcomb—
Shelburne

41.44
T Coxcomb—
Bishop and Coblentz

41.46
T Cockscomb—
Finley, plate 77

41.48
T Coxcomb—
Hall and Kretsinger, pg. 120

41.49
T Cactus Rose—
Bishop and Coblentz, pg. 74

41.51
T Unnamed—
Bishop and Coblentz, pg. 70

41.52
T Unnamed—
from a quilt in *Quilt Engagment
Calendar* 1982, plate 32

41.53
T Unnamed—
from a quilt ca. 1870 *Quilter's
Newsletter* 4/1992

41.54
T Flower Urn—
from a quilt ca. 1880
by Susan McCord in Greenfield
Village

41.551
T Potted Tulip—
Farm and Fireside 9/1929

41.552
T Pride of Iowa—
Hall and Kretsinger, pg. 242
Four Little Birds —
Shelburne (has 2 more birds)

41.56
T Egyptian Lotus Flower—
Hall and Kretsinger, pg. 198

41.6
T Unnamed—
Prudence Penny

41.72
T Urn—
Hall and Kretsinger, pg. 120

41.74
T Peony—
from a quilt by Whitehill in the
Denver Art Museum

41.8
T Unnamed—
Bresenhan/Texas

41.91
Rose—
Farmer's Wife 1932

41.93
Decorative Plant—
Nancy Cabot, *Chicago Tribune* 1935

41.95
D Rose Basket—
Rural New Yorker 1934

41.97
T Vase of Roses—
Sienkiewicz

41.99
T Democratic Rose—
Nancy Cabot, *Chicago Tribune* 1935

42.1
T Tulip Design—
Kansas City Star 2/5/1932

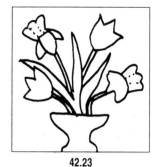

42.23
D Unnamed—
Needlecraft Magazine 1940

42.24
D Jonquils—
Nancy Cabot, *Chicago Tribune* 1933

42.25
D Nasturtiums—
Nancy Cabot, *Chicago Tribune* 1933

42.26
D Breath of Springtime—
Nancy Cabot, *Chicago Tribune* 1933

42.35
D Garden Bouquet—
Nancy Page (see as a series)

42.37
D Fragrance—
Nancy Cabot, *Chicago Tribune* 1933

42.41
T Cactus Rose—
Finley, pg. 66

42.43
T Unnamed—
from a quilt ca. 1870 in
Quilt Digest 1985

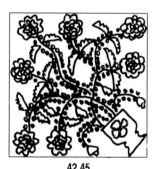

42.45
T Unnamed—
from a quilt dated 1886, collection:
A.Savage

42.46
T Unnamed—
from an album dated 1855

42.47
T Unnamed—
from an album dated 1848

42.48
T Unnamed—
from an album dated 1859

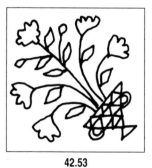

42.53
T Unnamed—
Prudence Penny

42.54
T French Provincial—
Nancy Cabot, *Chicago Tribune* 1935

42.55
T Lily Basket—
Nancy Cabot, *Chicago Tribune* 1936

42.56
T Basket of Flowers—
Nancy Cabot, *Chicago Tribune* 1935

42.58
T Tulip Basket—
Nancy Cabot, *Chicago Tribune* 1933

42.61
T Unnamed—
Modern Priscilla

42.623
T Unnamed—
from an album ca. 1850

42.625
T Unnamed—
Modern Priscilla 3/1926

42.634
D Wild Rose—
Ladies Art Company

42.635
D Rose Basket—
Nancy Cabot, *Chicago Tribune*

42.642
T Potted Rose—
Nancy Cabot, *Chicago Tribune* 1938

42.643
T Rose and Dahlia—
Nancy Cabot, *Chicago Tribune*

42.65
D Bleeding Hearts—
Sears 1934

42.66
D Flower Basket—
Webster in *Ladies Home Journal*
8/1911

42.67
T Unnamed—
from an album dated 1855

42.68
T Unnamed—
from an album dated 1853

42.692
T Rustic Basket—
inscribed on an album dated 1849

42.694
T Swiss Basket—
inscribed on an album dated 1840
These graceful wicker baskets are
typical of blocks in elaborate
Baltimore Album quilts

42.713
Decorated Basket—
Nancy Cabot, *Chicago Tribune* 1934

42.715
Flower Basket—
Carlie Sexton
Carlie Sexton's Basket—
Hall and Kretsinger, pg. 126

42.717
D Mrs. Halls Basket—
Hall and Kretsinger, pg. 126

42.72
D May Basket—
Kansas City Star 1946

42.732
D Flower Basket—
Ladies Art Company

42.733
D Basket of Daisies—
Hall and Kretsinger, pg. 126

42.735
D Flower Basket—
Nancy Cabot, *Chicago Tribune* 1933

42.742
D Flower Basket—
Nancy Cabot, *Chicago Tribune* 1935

42.743
D May Basket—
Needlecraft Magazine 1933

42.745
D Maude Hare's Basket—
Hall and Kretsinger, pg. 126

42.746
D Basket—
Farmer's Wife 1932

42.752
D French Basket—
Webster (alternates with scroll block)
Ivory Basket—
Mrs. Danner

42.754
D Basket Applique—
Kansas City Star 1935

42.756
D Unnamed—
Needlecraft 1923

42.76
D Basket of Roses—
Nancy Cabot, *Chicago Tribune* 1933

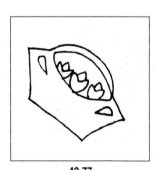

42.77
D Dutch Tulip Basket—
Nancy Cabot, *Chicago Tribune* 1933

42.78
D Garden Gift—
Needlecraft Magazine 2/1935 pg. 9

42.82
D Unnamed—
Aunt Martha ca. 1933

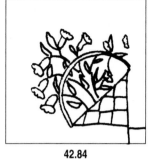

42.84
D Bells in Bloom—
Nancy Cabot, *Chicago Tribune* 1933

42.85
D Golden Poppies—
Nancy Cabot, *Chicago Tribune* 1933

42.91
D Iris in Baskets—
Webster

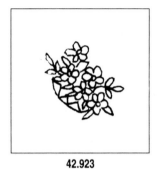

42.923
D Unnamed—
Aunt Martha ca. 1933

42.924
Bowl of Flowers—
Nancy Cabot, *Chicago Tribune* 1933

42.93
D Egyptian Lotus—
Nancy Cabot, *Chicago Tribune* 1935

42.94
D Blue Basket—
Paragon kit

42.95
D Fruit Bowl—
Nancy Cabot, *Chicago Tribune* 1935

42.96
D Vase of Posies—
Capper's Weekly ca. 1925

42.97
D Vase of Roses—
Nancy Cabot, *Chicago Tribune* 1934

42.992
D Tulip Garden—
Ladies Art Company #6071

42.993
D Tulip Garden—
Nancy Cabot, *Chicago Tribune* 1933

42.995
D Hearts and Flowers—
Nancy Cabot, *Chicago Tribune* 1934

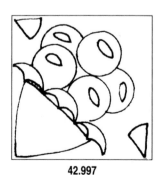

42.997
D Wax Flowers—
Nancy Cabot, *Chicago Tribune* 1937

43.12
Unnamed—
Ladies Art Company #878

43.14
Four Leaf Clover—
Kansas City Star 1947

43.16
Yellow Plume—
Nancy Cabot, *Chicago Tribune* 1936

43.22
T Oak Leaf—
Rural New Yorker

43.24
T Hop Vine—
name inscribed on a quilt ca. 1870
Shelburne

43.26
T Unnamed--
from an album dated 1857

43.28
T Ameranth—
from a quilt dated 1858 Indiana

43.33
T Trailing Vines—
Nancy Cabot, *Chicago Tribune* 1936

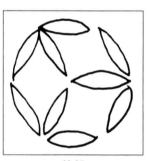

43.35
D Autumn Leaves—
Nancy Cabot, *Chicago Tribune* 1935

43.42
T Unnamed—
from an album dated 1851

43.43
T True Lover's Knot—
name inscribed on a quilt ca. 1870
Shelburne

43.45
T Unnamed—
from an album dated 1846

43.48
T Pride of the Forest—
Finley

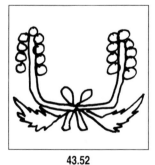

43.52
T Poke Berries—
name inscribed on a quilt ca. 1870
Shelburne #10.323

43.54
T Cherries—
Nancy Cabot, *Chicago Tribune* 1933

43.55
T Unnamed—
from an album dated 1848

43.62
T Unnamed—
from an album dated 1852

43.64
T Unnamed—
from an album dated 1856

43.65
T Unnamed—
from an album dated 1847

43.66
T Unnamed—
from an album dated 1857

43.72
T Cockscomb Variation—
from a quilt in *Quilt Engagement
Calendar* 1984, plate 31

43.74
T The Olive Branch—
Ladies Home Journal 1908

43.76
T Coxcomb—
Bishop and Coblentz

43.78
T Unnamed—
from a quilt ca. 1870 in
Quilt Engagement Calendar 1988,
plate 25

Other Symmetries/Floral Trees 44

43.82
T Tree of Life—
Bresenhan/Texas

43.83
T Tulip Pattern—
Vickery Publishing

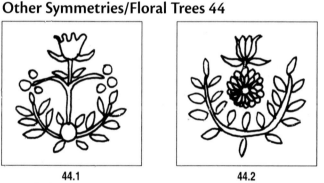

44.1
T Prairie Rose—
Rural New Yorker

44.2
T Tulip Design—
Ickis pg. 112

44.3
T Tulip Tree—
from a quilt ca. 1850
Spencer Museum

44.4
T Conventional Tulip—
Ickis, pg. 19

44.5
T Rose and Buds—
Nancy Cabot, *Chicago Tribune* 1937

44.6
T Prairie Flower—
Carlie Sexton

44.7

T Prairie Flower—
Hall and Kretsinger
Missouri Rose—
Hall and Kretsinger
Rose Tree—
Hall and Kretsinger

44.8

T Rambling Rose—
Bresenhan/Texas

44.9

T Unnamed—
from a quilt dated 1869,
Kansas Quilt Project

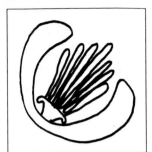

45.12

T Unnamed—
from a quilt ca. 1860

45.14

D Blue and White Quilt—
Ladies Home Journal 1908

45.16

D Sunlight and Shadows—
Nancy Cabot, *Chicago Tribune* 1936

45.18

D Tulip Garden—
Nancy Cabot, *Chicago Tribune* 1935

45.19

D Conventional Tulip—
Farmer's Wife 10/1929

45.23

D Pink Rose—
Webster (see also 31.93)
Rose with Watermelon Border—
Mrs. Danner

45.24

D Rose of Sharon—
Ladies Art Company #44

45.26

T Kentucky Rose—
Ladies Art Company #42

45.28

T Rose of LeMoyne—
Nancy Cabot, *Chicago Tribune* 1935

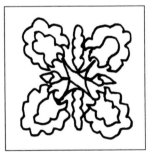

45.32

Sweet Pea—
Nancy Cabot, *Chicago Tribune* 1934

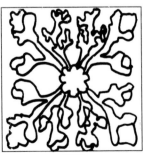

45.34

T The Poppy—
Finley, pg. 65

45.36

T Unnamed—
Comfort

45.38

T Unnamed—
from an album dated 1844

45.42
T True Lover's Knot—
Omaha World Herald 1912
Conventional Scroll—
Nancy Cabot, *Chicago Tribune*
A Kansas Pattern—
Whitehill in Denver Art Museum

45.44
T Unnamed—
from an album dated 1847

45.5
T Unnamed—
from an album dated 1847

45.6
T Unnamed—
from an album dated 1847

45.72
T Persian Palm Lily—
Ladies Art Company #52

45.74
T Unnamed—
from an album dated 1860

45.79
Hunter's Horn—
Hearth and Home

45.81
T Unnamed—
from an album dated 1845

45.82
D Gay Garden—
Webster ca. 1925

45.83
T Unnamed—
from an album dated 1844

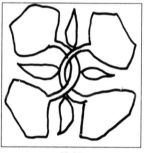

45.85
D Jerusalem Cross—
Nancy Cabot, *Chicago Tribune* 1934

45.86
T Rose of LeMoyne—
Nancy Cabot, *Chicago Tribune* 1933

45.87
T Old Fashioned Rose—
Hall and Kretsinger pg. 111

45.88
T Unnamed—
from an album dated 1863

45.92
T Unnamed—
from an album dated 1854

45.94
D Swedona Block—
Nancy Cabot, *Chicago Tribune* 1938

46.12
D Adam and Eve—
Nancy Cabot, *Chicago Tribune* 1934
Garden of Eden—
Nancy Cabot, *Chicago Tribune* 1937

46.14
D Peaches—
Nancy Cabot, *Chicago Tribune* 1934

46.16
D Maude Hare's Flower Garden—
Hall and Kretsinger, pg. 107

46.22
D Autumn Fruit—
Farm Journal 1936

46.24
D Victory Garden—
Wheeler/Brooks #7516

46.31
T Strawberry—
Hall and Kretsinger

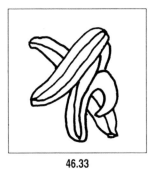

46.33
D Banana—
block from the Horn of Plenty series
#73.8

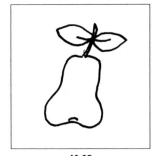

46.35
D Pear—
block from the Garden Fruit series
#73.9

46.41
T Pineapple Design—
Webster, fig. 52
Modern Pineapple—
Mrs. Danner

46.42
T The Pineapple—
Needlecraft Magazine May, 1928

46.44
T Pineapple—
Nancy Cabot, *Chicago Tribune* 1933

46.45
T Pineapple—
Ickis, pg. 82

46.46
T Unnamed—
from a quilt in the *Quilt Engagement Calendar* 1978, plate 56

46.47
T Pieced Pineapple—
Finley plate 80

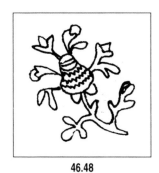

46.48
T Unnamed—
from a quilt in Lasansky,
Pieced by Mother, pg. 56

46.49
T Unnamed—
from an album dated 1860

46.61

T Love Apple—
Finley and Carlie Sexton

46.62

T Love Apple—
Hall and Kretsinger pg. 106

46.63

T Love Apple—
Nancy Cabot, *Chicago Tribune* 1933

46.64

T Love Apple—
McKim

46.65

T California Rose—
Aunt Martha

46.66

T Rose of LeMoyne—
Hall and Kretsinger, pg. 114

46.68

T Unnamed—
Ladies Circle Patchwork Quilts,
Spring 1984

46.69

T The Peach—
Comfort

46.72

T Temperance Ball—
Carlie Sexton, Old Fashioned Quilts

46.74

T Pomegranate—
Mountain Mist

46.76

T Unnamed—
Safford and Bishop, pg. 188

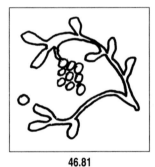

46.81

T Unnamed—
from an album dated 1847

46.83

T Grapes—
Nancy Cabot, *Chicago Tribune* 1934

46.86

T Wild Grape—
Comfort

46.88

T Unnamed—
Lasansky, *Pennsylvania Papers*

46.89

T Wild Cherries—
Hearth and Home

47.11
D Sunbonnet Baby—
Quilt World February, 1977

47.12
D Sunbonnet Sue—
Mrs. Danner

47.13
D Sunbonnet Susie—
Nancy Cabot, *Chicago Tribune* 1940

47.14
D Sunbonnet Baby—
Nancy Cabot, *Chicago Tribune*

47.15
D Sunbonnet Sue—
Ladies Art Company 1900–1925

47.16
D Sunbonnet Baby—
Rainbow 1932

47.17
D Little Dutch Girl—
Frank's

47.22
D Sunbonnet Sue—
Eveline Foland in
Kansas City Star 1930

47.24
D Mary Ann—
Nancy Cabot, *Chicago Tribune* 1933

47.26
D Mary Lou—
Nancy Cabot, *Chicago Tribune*

47.28
D Remember—
Eveline Johnson,
Needlecraft Magazine 1936

47.32
D Unnamed—
Ordell, early 20th century

47.33
D Flower Girl—
Sears, Roebuck and Co., 1934
(alternates with #53.44)

47.37
D Sunbonnet Girl—
Workbasket, April, 1977

47.42
D Sunbonnet Sue—
Jinny Beyer in *Quilter's Newsletter
Magazine* March, 1975

47.44
D Unnamed—
unknown clipping

47.48
D Dutch Girl—
Nancy Cabot, *Chicago Tribune* 1933

47.52
D Calico Girls—
Nancy Cabot, *Chicago Tribune*
(Cabot had many variations
of this figure)

47.54
D Old Fashioned Lady—
Aunt Martha

47.56
D Bride Quilt—
Aunt Martha

47.57
D Old Fashioned Girl—
Wheeler/Brooks #798

47.58
D Colonial Ladies—
Vogue

47.61
D Unnamed—
Needlecraft Magazine 1932

47.63
D Unnamed—
Sears, Roebuck and Co., 1934

47.65
D Unnamed—
Rainbow

47.67
D Sunbonnet Girls Running
Between the Raindrops—
Wheeler/Brooks #7144

47.72
D Balloon Girl—
Wheeler/Brooks #709

47.74
D Balloon Girl—
Wheeler/Brooks

47.82
D Sunbonnet Girl—
Wheeler/Brooks #7337

47.84
D Old Fashioned Girl in a Swing—
Wheeler/Brooks #723

47.86
D Sunbonnet Sue—
Wheeler/Brooks #5025A

47.9
D Colonial Lady—
Grandma Dexter.
See as a series #74.21

48.12
D Overall Bill—
Ladies Art Company 1900–1925

48.13
D Overall Boy—
Frank's

48.16
D Straw Hat Boy—
Mrs. Danner

48.17
D Dutch Boy—
Nancy Cabot, *Chicago Tribune* 1942

48.22
D Sunny Jim—
Nancy Cabot, *Chicago Tribune* 1933

48.24
D Farmer Boy—
Frank's

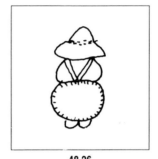

48.26
D Unnamed—
Sears, Roebuck and Co. 1934
(alternates with #55.82)

48.28
D Recollect—
Eveline Johnson in
Needlecraft Magazine 1938

48.32
D Overall Andy—
McKim, *Designs Worth Doing* #473

48.36
D Overall Andy—
McKim, *Designs Worth Doing* #473

48.4
D Romper Boy—
Rainbow

48.52
D Fisher Lad—
Wheeler/Brooks

48.54
D Fisher Boy—
Wheeler/Brooks #5025

48.6
D Happy Jack—
Nancy Cabot, *Chicago Tribune* 1936

48.7
D Farmer Boy—
Hagerman attributes to
duBarry ca. 1935

48.8
D Unnamed—
Hagerman pg. 31

49.12
D Cowgirl—
Aunt Ellen (Aunt Martha)

49.13
D Cowboy—
Aunt Ellen (Aunt Martha)

49.15
D Cowboy and Horse—
Wheeler/Brooks #770 (these were
sold as a series and individually;
there were more in the series than
are pictured here)

49.16
D Cowboy and Horse—
Wheeler/Brooks #770

49.17
D Cowboy—
Wheeler/Brooks #7025 and 7131

49.18
D Cowboy and Horse—
Wheeler/Brooks #7353

49.22
D Bronco Buster—
Needlecraft Magazine 1929

49.24
D Wild West Quilt—
Wheeler/Brooks #7566

49.32
T Unnamed—
from a quilt ca. 1900 from
Pennsylvania

49.34
D Squaw Quilt—
Hagerman #W-65

49.35
D Indian Princess—
Betty Royal in *Stitch 'n Sew* 8/1983

49.42
D Aunt Jemima—
from a quilt ca. 1935

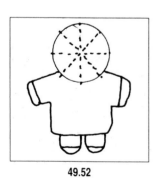

49.52
D Unnamed—
from a quilt ca. 1933

49.54
D Acrobats—
Nancy Cabot, *Chicago Tribune* 1937

49.61
D Dutch Lass—
Nancy Cabot, *Chicago Tribune* 1938

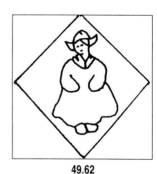

49.62
D Dutch Girls—
Wheeler/Brooks #2054

Human Figures/Costumed Figures 49

49.63
D Dutch Boy—
Wheeler/Brooks #2054

49.64
D Toy Soldiers—
Wheeler/Brooks #7148

49.66
D Little Dutch Boy—
Nancy Cabot, *Chicago Tribune* 1933

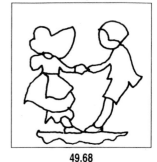

49.68
D Dutch Boy and Girl—
Nancy Cabot, *Chicago Tribune* 1935

49.72
D Bo Peep—
McKim, *Designs Worth Doing* #265

49.73
D Boy Blue—
McKim, *Designs Worth Doing* #264

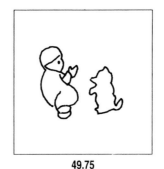

49.75
D Unnamed—
Sophie LaCroix

49.78
D Early to Bed—
Nancy Cabot, *Chicago Tribune* 1935

Miscellaneous Humans 50

49.82
D Paper Doll—
Wheeler/Brooks

49.85
D Dotty, the Paper Doll Girl—
Woman's Home Companion 1931

49.86
D Dicky, the Paper Doll Boy—
Woman's Home Companion 1931

50.1
T Unnamed—
from an album dated 1854

50.2
T Unnamed—
from an album dated 1844

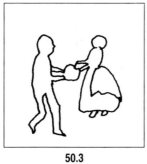

50.3
T Adam and Eve—
from a quilt ca. 1875

50.4
T The Creation of the Animals—
from a quilt by Harriett Powers ca.
1898 in the Smithsonian Institution

50.8
Hallowe'en Block—
Ladies Art Company #496

51.12
D Butterfly—
Nancy Cabot, *Chicago Tribune* 1933

51.14
D Fancy Butterfly—
Grandmother Clark

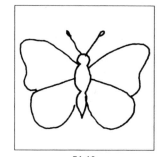

51.16
D Plain Butterfly—
Grandmother Clark

51.18
D Butterfly—
Boag

51.22
D Butterfly—
Wheeler/Brooks #C515

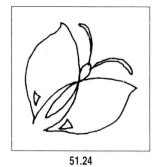

51.24
D Butterfly—
Nancy Cabot, *Chicago Tribune* 1936

51.26
D Butterfly—
Rainbow

51.28
D Butterflies—
Wheeler/Brooks #768

51.32
D Butterflies—
Wheeler/Brooks #768

51.34
D Butterfly Applique—
Wheeler/Brooks #7462

51.35
D Gay Butterflies—
Wheeler/Brooks

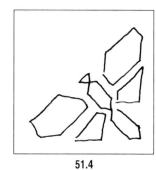

51.4
D Firefly—
Nancy Cabot, *Chicago Tribune* 1936

51.52
D Unnamed—
McCall's Needlework

51.54
D Butterfly and Flower—
Wheeler/Brooks 7246

51.62
D Butterfly Garden—
Rainbow #713

51.64
D Unnamed—
Rainbow #725

Other Symmetries/Butterflies 51

51.66
D Morning Glories—
Rainbow #731 and #847

51.68
D Four Poppies and Butterflies—
Rainbow #808

51.69
D Unnamed—
Rainbow #728

51.72
T Butterfly—
Rural New Yorker

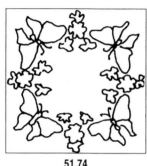

51.74
D Butterfly—
Ladies Art Company #6007

51.76
D Butterflies—
Ladies Art Company #414

51.78
T Unnamed—
from an album dated 1850

51.8
D Butterflies—
from a quilt ca. 1935 Woodard and
Greenstein/20th Century pg. 66

Birds 52–54

52.12
D Dove Applique—
Wheeler/Brooks

52.14
T Flying Bird—
Wilkinson

52.15
T Bluebird—
Nancy Cabot, *Chicago Tribune* 1944

52.16
D Unnamed—
Sears, Roebuck and Co. 1934

52.17
D Unnamed—
Rainbow #452

52.18
T Unnamed—
from an album dated 1847

52.19
D Bluebird Quilt—
Wheeler/Brooks

52.22
D Bird Quilt—
Wheeler/Brooks

52.24
D Curious Chicks—
Modern Priscilla 1926 (alternates
with a flower)

52.25
D Robin—
Nancy Cabot, *Chicago Tribune* 1934

52.26
D Red Bird—
Nancy Cabot, *Chicago Tribune* 1935

52.27
D Scarlet Song Bird—
Nancy Cabot, *Chicago Tribune*

52.28
T Pennsylvania Dutch Design—
Ickis, pg. 104

52.3
D Dickey Bird—
Wheeler/Brooks

52.42
D Yellow Warbler—
Rainbow #909F

52.44
D Cardinal and Morning Glory—
Rainbow #843

52.46
D Apple Blossoms—
Rainbow #858C

52.52
T Unnamed—
from an album dated 1854

52.54
T Unnamed—
from an album dated 1854

52.55
T Unnamed—
from a quilt in Bresenhan and
Puentes (Ark #59.4 is in center)

52.57
T Unnamed—
from an album dated 1849

52.59
T Unnamed—
from an album dated 1848

52.62
T Unnamed—
from an album dated 1861

52.64
T Unnamed—
from an album dated 1852

52.72
T Birds and Blossoms—
from a quilt in the
Quilt Engagement Calendar 1977,
plate 54

52.74
D Mr. Owl
Nancy Cabot, *Chicago Tribune*
Owl Block—
Nancy Cabot, *Chicago Tribune*
Wise Old Owl—
Nancy Cabot, *Chicago Tribune* 1938

52.76
D Owls in Applique—
Wheeler/Brooks #7508

52.82
T Two Doves—
unknown clipping
Bluebird—
Comfort

52.84
T Sweetheart Design—
Comfort

52.86
T Birds and Basket—
Comfort

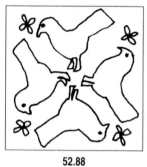

52.88
T Unnamed—
from an album dated 1847

52.92
T Heart and Dove—
from a quilt ca. 1890
from Ulster, Ireland
Heart and Spade—
both names in use in Ulster

Poultry 53

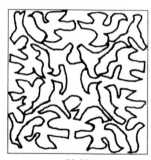

52.94
T Bluebird Design—
New York Press July 12, 1914

53.12
T Unnamed—
from an album dated 1865

53.14
D Little Chanticlear—
Nancy Cabot, *Chicago Tribune* 1938

53.16
D Unnamed—
Aunt Martha, *Prize-Winning Quilts*

53.18
D Chanticleer—
Mountain Mist #G

53.19
T Unnamed—
from an album dated 1854

53.22
D Chick in Boots—
Nancy Cabot, *Chicago Tribune* 1936

53.24
D Baby Chick—
Nancy Cabot, *Chicago Tribune* 1934

53.32
T Unnamed—
from an album dated 1865

53.35
D Ducky Coverlet—
Farmer's Wife 6/1934

53.38
Wild Ducks—
Mountain Mist #45

53.42
D Just Ducky—
Wheeler/Brooks

53.44
D Ducky Doo—
Sears, Roebuck and Co. 1934
(alternates with #47.33)

53.46
D Unnamed—
Needlecraft Magazine 1929

53.52
D Unnamed—
Needlecraft Magazine 1932

53.53
D Unnamed—
Needlecraft Magazine 1932

53.6
D Flamingoes—
Nancy Cabot, *Chicago Tribune* 1936

53.72
D Mother Goose—
Nancy Cabot, *Chicago Tribune* 1934

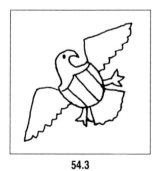

53.74
D A Pair of Geese—
Nancy Cabot, *Chicago Tribune* 1934
A Pair of Ducklings—
Nancy Cabot, *Chicago Tribune* 1938

53.8
D Turkey and Pumpkin—
Wheeler/Brooks #5901N

Birds/Eagles 54

54.22
T Unnamed—
from an album dated 1855

54.23
T Unnamed—
from an album

54.3
T Unnamed—
from a quilt dated 1917
(see #86.3)

54.4
T Unnamed—
from an album dated 1850

Birds/Eagles 54

54.5
T Unnamed—
from an album dated 1853

54.6
T Unnamed—
from an album dated 1852

54.72
T Eagle Applique—
Peto, *American Quilts*, pg. 42

54.8
T Unnamed—
from an album dated 1849

Dogs 55

55.13
D Unnamed—
Needlecraft Magazine 1929

55.15
D Scottie—
Needlecraft Magazine 1935

55.22
D Scottie—
Nancy Cabot, *Chicago Tribune* 1934

55.24
D Scottie Dog—
Wheeler/Brooks #1517

55.26
D Scotch Terriers—
Wheeler/Brooks #7145

55.28
D Humoristic Cat and Dog—
Vogue #2054

55.32
D Blue Ribbon Setter—
Nancy Cabot, *Chicago Tribune* 1936

55.35
D Frisky Dog—
Wheeler/Brooks

55.42
D Scottie—
Wheeler/Brooks
Puppy Applique—
Wheeler/Brooks #520

55.43
D Wirehaired Pup—
Nancy Cabot, *Chicago Tribune* 1935

55.51
D Puppy Blocks—
Wheeler/Brooks #7438

55.52
D Unnamed—
Sears, Roebuck and Co. 1934
(alternates with #48.26)

55.53
D Little Bowser—
Nancy Cabot, *Chicago Tribune* 1935

55.54
D Doggie Applique—
Wheeler/Brooks #1846

55.55
D Dog Applique—
Wheeler/Brooks #2216

55.56
D Puppies—
Wheeler/Brooks #7260

Cats, Rabbits, Fish, etc. 56

56.11
D Kitten—
Nancy Cabot, *Chicago Tribune* 1934

56.12
D Kitten Applique—
Wheeler/Brooks #5963

56.13
D Calico Cat—
Wheeler/Brooks #1583

56.14
D Kitten Block—
Nancy Cabot, *Chicago Tribune* 1938

56.15
D Kitten—
Wheeler/Brooks #7260

56.16
D Nursery Patch—
Wheeler/Brooks

56.17
D Kitten Applique—
Wheeler/Brooks #1988

56.18
D Breakfast—
Nancy Cabot, *Chicago Tribune* 1938

56.2
D Teddy Bear—
Wheeler/Brooks #2916

56.23
D Teddy Bear—
Wheeler/Brooks

56.26
D Teddy Bear—
Nancy Cabot, *Chicago Tribune* 1934

56.32
D Appliqued Bunny—
Wilkinson

56.33
D Bunny Applique—
Wheeler/Brooks #1876

56.34
D Peter Rabbit in his Garden—
Nancy Cabot, *Chicago Tribune*

56.35
D Jack Rabbit—
Nancy Cabot, *Chicago Tribune* 1938

56.37
D Bunnies—
Webster design 1914
(alternates with basket)

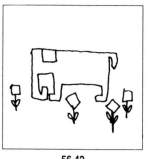

56.42
D Elephant—
Needlecraft Magazine 1929

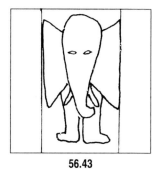

56.43
D Little Jumbo—
Nancy Cabot, *Chicago Tribune* 1935

56.44
D Old Jumbo—
Nancy Cabot, *Chicago Tribune* 1938

56.45
D Elephant Applique—
Wheeler/Brooks #1621

56.46
D Dancing Jumbo—
Nancy Cabot, *Chicago Tribune* 1936

56.47
D Elephant—
Nancy Cabot, *Chicago Tribune* 1935

56.48
D Lucky Elephant—
Vogue #2053

56.52
D Buddy Squirrel—
Nancy Cabot, *Chicago Tribune* 1934
Papa Squirrel—
Nancy Cabot, *Chicago Tribune* 1938

56.54
D Little Omar—
Nancy Cabot, *Chicago Tribune* 1938

56.55
D Lamb—
Nancy Cabot, *Chicago Tribune* 1934

56.58
D Hobby Horse—
Nancy Cabot, *Chicago Tribune* 1938

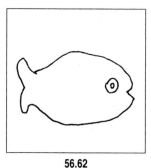

56.62
D Jonah's Fish—
Nancy Cabot, *Chicago Tribune* 1936

Cats, Rabbits, Fish, etc. 56

56.64
D Baby Shark—
Nancy Cabot, *Chicago Tribune* 1936

56.66
D Bias Tape Motif—
Wheeler/Brooks #7400

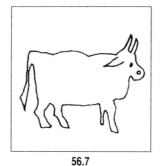

56.7
T Unnamed—
from an album dated 1857

56.8
T Unnamed—
from an album dated 1865

Trees 57

56.9
T Unnamed—
from an album dated 1854

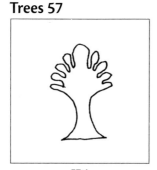

57.1
T Forest Bride's Quilt—
from a quilt dated 1861
in the Art Institute of Chicago

57.3
T Unnamed—
from a quilt in the
Quilt Engagement Calendar 1978,
plate 39

57.4
D Trees and Garlands—
alternates with wreath in Paragon kit

57.5
T Tree of Life—
from a quilt ca. 1850 in
Quilts of Tennessee, pg. 50

57.6
T Cherry Trees—
Paragon kit, a copy of a quilt ca.
1850 in the Art Institute of Chicago

57.7
D Evergreen Tree—
Nancy Cabot, *Chicago Tribune* 1936

57.8
D Palm Tree—
Nancy Cabot, *Chicago Tribune*

Houses and Buildings 58

57.92
D Sheltering Pines—
Nancy Cabot, *Chicago Tribune* 1936

57.94
D Monday's Trees—
Nancy Cabot, *Chicago Tribune* 1936

58.12
D Unnamed—
Needlecraft Magazine

58.13
D Unnamed—
Needlecraft Magazine 1923

Other Symmetries/Houses and Buildings 58

58.14
D Unnamed—
Needlecraft Magazine 1923

58.15
D Sunnyside—
Modern Priscilla August, 1928

58.16
D Enchanted Cottage—
Wheeler/Brooks #726

58.17
D Homestead—
Wheeler/Brooks #1576
Little Village—
Wheeler/Brooks #1576

58.18
D The Cottage Behind the Hill—
Aunt Martha, *Prize-Winning Quilts*

58.2
D Unnamed—
Sears, Roebuck and Co., 1934

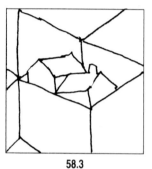

58.3
D House and Hill—
Nancy Cabot, *Chicago Tribune*

58.4
T Unnamed—
from an album dated 1852

Boats 58

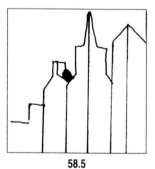

58.5
D Skyscraper—
Successful Farming

59.13
D Red Sails—
Nancy Cabot, *Chicago Tribune*

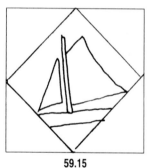

59.15
D Sailboat—
Wheeler/Brooks #1549

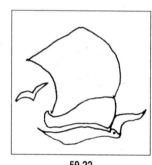

59.22
D The Sea Gull—
Needlecraft Magazine 1933

59.24
D Dream Ship—
Nancy Cabot, *Chicago Tribune* 1935

59.25
D Treasure Ship—
Needlecraft Magazine 1935

59.3
T Unnamed—
from an album dated 1849

59.4
T Unnamed—
from a quilt in Bresenhan and
Puentes, combined with dove
#52.55

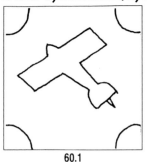

60.1

D The Airplane—
Nancy Cabot, *Chicago Tribune*

60.22

D Bedtime—
Nancy Cabot, *Chicago Tribune* 1936

60.24

T Unnamed—
from an album dated 1846

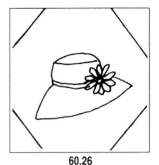

60.26

D Unnamed—
Wheeler/Brooks

60.32

T Unnamed—
from an album dated 1853

60.35

T Unnamed—
from an album dated 1865

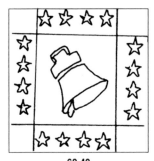

60.42

D Centennial—
Nancy Cabot, *Chicago Tribune*

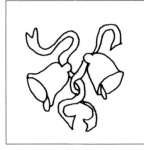

60.44

D Bells of St. Mary's—
Nancy Cabot, *Chicago Tribune* 1939

60.51

T Unnamed—
from an album dated 1865

60.53

T The Valentine Quilt—
Kansas City Star 1955

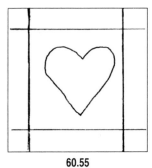

60.55

D The Bleeding Heart—
Kansas City Star 1950

60.56

T Gift of Love—
Finley, pg. 190

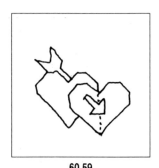

60.59

D Valentines—
Nancy Cabot, *Chicago Tribune* 1936

60.62

T Unnamed—
from an album dated 1850

60.64

T Unnamed—
from an album dated 1852

60.66

T Unnamed—
from an album dated 1865

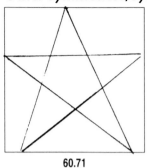

60.71
D Eastern Star—
Nancy Cabot, *Chicago Tribune* 1935

60.72
T Unnamed—
from an album dated 1852

60.74
T Unnamed—
from an album dated 1860

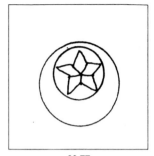

60.77
T Star and Crescent—
Wilkinson

60.78
T Crescent Moon—
Hearth and Home

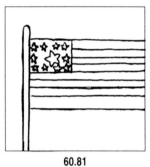

60.81
T Unnamed—
from an album dated 1865

60.82
T Unnamed—
from an album dated 1861

60.83
T Unnamed—
from an album dated 1859

60.84
T Unnamed—
from an album dated 1867

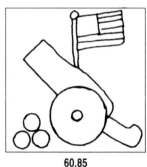

60.85
D Fourth of July—
Nancy Cabot, *Chicago Tribune* 1936

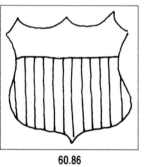

60.86
T Shield—
Ladies Art Company #420

60.87
T Unnamed—
from an album dated 1859

60.88
T Unnamed—
from an album dated 1861

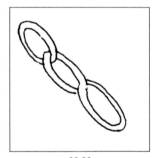

60.92
T Unnamed—
from an album ca. 1860
(Odd Fellow's Chain)

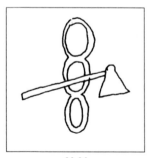

60.94
T Unnamed—
from an album ca. 1850
(Odd Fellow's Chain)

60.96
T Unnamed—
from a quilt ca. 1858
(Masonic symbol)

71.3 D Falling Leaves—Nancy Page 1936 (18 leaves) See #43

72.1 D Four Flowers Set—
Wheeler/Brooks
(3 flowers pictured)

71.5 D Leaf Quilt—Nancy Page 1931
(4 leaves) See #5.1

72.2 D Flower Garden—Home Art (10 flowers)
Aunt Susan's Flower Garden—Home Art

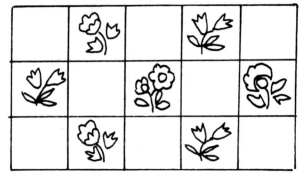

72.3 D Coverlet in Floral Design—*Needlecraft Magazine* 1934 (4 flowers)

72.5 D Laurel Wreath—Nancy Page 1934 (30 blocks)

72.4 D French Bouquet—Nancy Page 1933 (12 bouquets, 15 border blocks)

Bouquets 72

72.6 D Hearts and Flowers—
Nancy Page 1938 (4 blocks)

72.7 D Modernistic Flower—*Portland Oregonian* (28 blocks)

72.82 D Unnamed—Rainbow stamped block
set #500v (12 blocks) See #34.75

Containers, Fruit and Wreaths 73

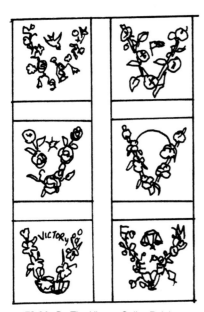

72.84 D The Victory Quilt—Rainbow
stamped block ca. 1943 (6 blocks)

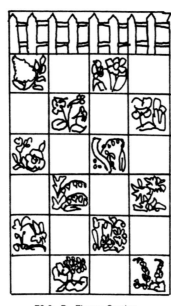

72.9 D Flower Garden—
McKim 1929–1930 (25 blocks)

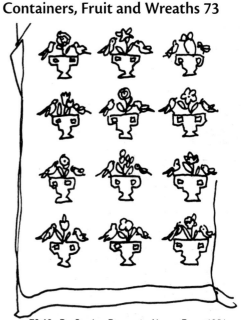

73.12 D Garden Bouquet—Nancy Page 1931
(20 blocks) See 42.35

73.13 D Quilt of Birds—
Needlecraft Magazine 1937

73.2 D Flower Basket—Aunt Martha (12 blocks)

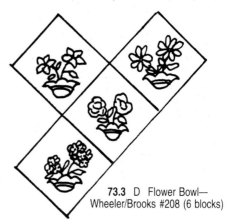

73.3 D Flower Bowl—
Wheeler/Brooks #208 (6 blocks)

73.4 D Memory Bouquet—Eveline Foland 1930
(20 blocks in *Kansas City Star*, 25 in *Detroit News*)

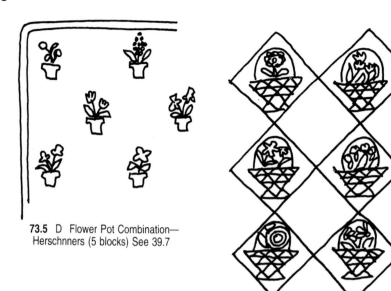

73.5 D Flower Pot Combination—
Herschnners (5 blocks) See 39.7

73.6 D Fruit Basket Quilt—McKim 1929–1930 (32 baskets)

73.7 D Grandmother's Garden—Nancy Page 1928 (20 baskets)

73.82 D Horn of Plenty—Eveline Foland in *Kansas City Star* 1932 (18 fruits)

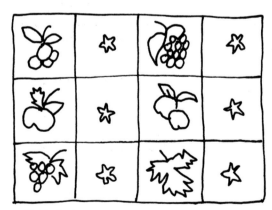

73.84 D Garden Fruits—Nancy Page 1935 (10 fruits)

73.9 T Wreath—Nancy Page 1931 (4)

74.12 D Sunbonnet Sue—McKim/Designs Worth Doing (3 figures)

74.13 D Children's Nursery Blocks—Rainbow stamped block set #715 (6 figures)

74.15 D Sunbonnet Babies—Herschnners #3581 (12 figures)

74.17 D Mother Goose Quilt—Nancy Page 1938 (9 figures)

74.18 D Sunbonnet Girl—Grandma Dexter (6 figures)

74.19 D Overall Boy—Grandma Dexter (6 figures)

74.21 D Colonial Lady—Grandma Dexter (6 figures) See 47.9

74.23 D Sunbonnet Girls—Wheeler/Brooks #7027

74.25 D Colonial Belle—*Capper's Weekly* (12 blocks)

74.3 D 1-2 Buckle My Shoe—Nancy Page 1937 (10 blocks)

74.4 D Mother Goose—McKim (12 blocks)

74.5 D Bible Quilt—*Ladies Home Journal* #1503 (12 blocks)

74.6 D Little Brown KoKo—*Capper's Weekly*

Objects and Animals 75

75.13 D Story Book Quilt—Marion Cheever Whiteside in *McCalls* (12 blocks)

75.15 D Three Little Kittens—Ladies Art Company #6068 (8 blocks)

75.17 D Pussy Cat—Herschnner

75.23 D Crib Cover—Famous Features #2732

75.24 D Crib of Sleepy Time Pets—*Capper's Weekly* 1935 (8 blocks)

75.26 D Animal Crib Quilt—Wheeler/Brooks #7009

75.3 D Three Little Pigs—McKim 1934 (13 blocks)

75.4 D Teddy Bear—Herschnner #3613

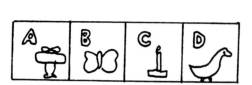

75.51 D ABC Quilt—Boag kit 1933 (24 blocks)

75.52 D Toy Shop Window—McKim 1933–1934 (12 blocks)

75.54 D Alphabet Quilt—Nancy Page 1929 (24 blocks)

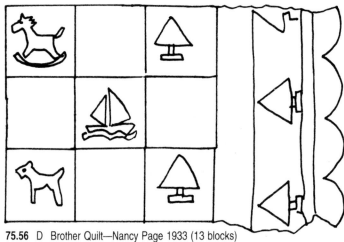

75.56 D Brother Quilt—Nancy Page 1933 (13 blocks)

75.57 D Sister Quilt—Nancy Page 1933 (13 blocks)

75.59 D Christmas Toy Quilt—Aileen Bullard in *Kansas City Star* 1932 (13 blocks)

75.62 D Quilt of Birds—Nancy Page 1937 (12 birds)

75.64 D Birds—*Quilter's Newsletter Magazine* ca 1973 (4 birds)

75.68 D Audubon or Bird Life Quilt—McKim 1928–1929

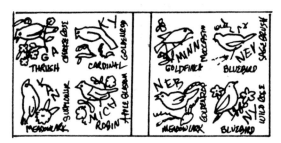

75.66 D Official State Birds and Flower—Rainbow

75.72 D Calendar Quilt—Nancy Page 1935 (12 months)

75.74 D Old Almanac—Nancy Page 1932 (12 signs)

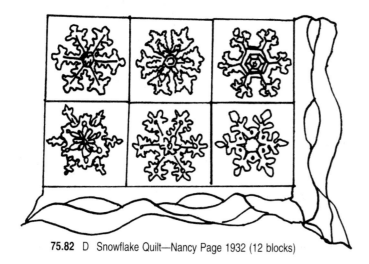

75.82 D Snowflake Quilt—Nancy Page 1932 (12 blocks)

75.9 D Sunflower Bedspread—attributed to John Then in *McCalls*

75.84 D Pretty Snowflake—Rainbow stamped block set #733 (6 blocks) See also snowflakes numbered 36.6

80.11 D Flower Garden—Lockport

80.12 D Floral Basket—*Needlecraft Magazine*

80.14 D Old Fashioned May Basket—*Needlecraft Magazine*

80.15 D Spring Basket—*Needlecraft Magazine*
Spring Bouquet—Herschnner

Dogwood Basket image

80.13 D Dogwood Basket—Ladies Art Company

Lady Sheridan image

80.16 D Lady Sheridan—Home Needlecraft Creations

80.17 D The Applique Basket—Anne Orr

80.22 T Indiana Wreath—*McCalls* ca. 1935

80.23　T　Indiana Wreath—name inscribed on quilt dated 1858 in Webster

80.24　D　June Basket—Home Needlecraft Creations kit #7168

80.31　D　Basket of Roses—Mrs. Danner Books 1 & 2

80.33　D　Unnamed—from a quilt ca. 1935 in *Quilt Engagement Calendar* 1992, plate 19

80.34　D　Poppy Basket—Boag kit

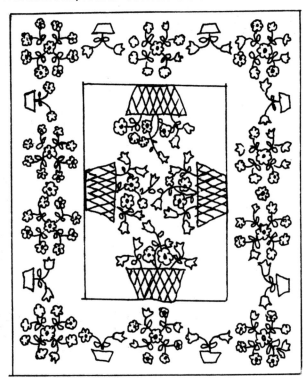

80.41 D Cape Cod Basket—Source not found

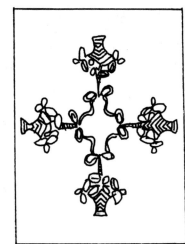

80.42 D Poppy Basket—Ladies Art Company

80.43 D French Basket—St. Louis Fancy Work

80.44 D Pink Dogwood in Baskets—Webster

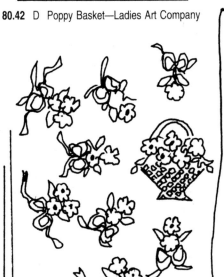

80.46 D Baskets and Wild Roses—St. Louis Fancy Work

80.47 D Garland and Basket—Ann Orr in *Good Housekeeping*

80.48 D Four Baskets—*Needlecraft Magazine*

80.49 D Poinsettia—Mountain Mist

81.1 D Crib Quilt Design—*Modern Priscilla* 1924

81. 2 D American Beauty—*McCalls*

81.23 D Poppy—*Capper's Weekly*

81.4 D Sunflower—*Capper's Weekly*

81.5 D Daisy Chain—*Mary McElwain* 1936

81.63 D First Lady—
Needlecraft Supply

81.65 D American Beauty Bouquet—Gold Art Needlework,
also Homeneedlecraft Creations #7452

81.71 D Orchid Wreath—Rose Kretsinger in Hall and Kretsinger

81.73 D Morning Glory—Webster

81.75 D Morning Glory—Webster

81.76 T Tulip Wreath—*Ladies Home Journal 1912* Conventional Flower Design—*Modern Priscilla* 1925

81.77 D Morning Glories—Nancy Cabot, *Chicago Tribune* 1935

81.81 D Unnamed—*Woman's World*

81.92 T Wreath of Roses—Hall and Kretsinger pg. 187

81.94 T Wreath and Star—Ickis pg. 24

82.13 D Climbing Rose—Herschnner kit

82.15 D Old Fashioned Bouquet—Ladies Art Company #6080

82.17 D White House Quilt—*Needlecraft Magazine* 1937
Cape Cod Quilt—*McCalls* Lady Delano—Homeneedlecraft Creations

82.21 D Marie Antoinette—Herschnner

82.22 D Spring Bouquet—Needlecraft kit #3575   **82.23** D Pansy Bed—Needlecraft kit #3576   **82.24** D Rose Bouquet—Herschnner

82.25 D Formal Garden—Needlecraft kit #3555

82.26 D Old Fashioned Spray—Anne Orr in *Good Housekeeping*

82.27 D Rose and Bowknot—Anne Orr in *Good Housekeeping*

82.28 D Old Sampler Quilt—Anne Orr in *Good Housekeeping* 1937

82.29 D Unnamed—from a quilt ca. 1940 (probably a kit)

82.31 D Pansy—McKim/*101 Quilt Patterns*, pg. 97

82.32 D Pansies—*Capper's Weekly*

82.33 D Pansy—Progress kit #1365

82.41 D Poppy Wreath—Mountain Mist

82.42 D Poppy—Anne Orr in *Good Housekeeping*

82.44 D Painted Poppies—Mountain Mist

82.46 D Poppy Design—Webster

82.48 D Poppy—Boag kit

82.51 D Climbing Rose—Lockport Batting

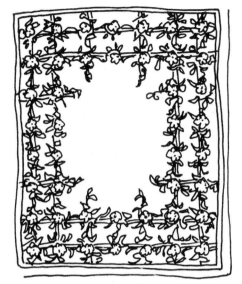

82.54 D Unnamed—
Nancy Cabot, *Chicago Tribune* 1935

82.62 D Unnamed—Bucilla kit

82.63 D Morning Glory—*McCalls* 1928

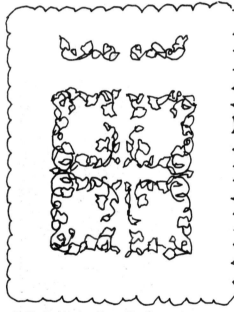

82.65 D Morning Glory—Mrs. Danner Books 1 & 2

82.66 D Morning Glory Vine Scroll—Needlecraft kit

82.711 D The Sunflower—Mountain Mist

82.712 D The Sunflower Quilt—Webster

82.72 D Tiger Lily—from a quilt ca. 1940
in Clark/Ohio, pg. 104

82.73 D Gladiola—from a quilt 1946
in Nebraska, pg. 46

82.74 D Carnation—from a quilt ca. 1940 in *Quilt Engagement Calendar* 1992, plate 57 (probably a Progress kit)

82.75 D The Iris—Anne Orr

82.76 D Iris Applique—Herschnner kit

82.77 D Spring—Boag kit

82.78 D April Showers—Mountain Mist #82

82.79 D The Garden—from a quilt 1857 in Finley, plate 57

82.81 D Provincial—Paragon kit

82.82 D Cluster of Roses—Webster

82.83 D Rose of Sharon—Mountain Mist

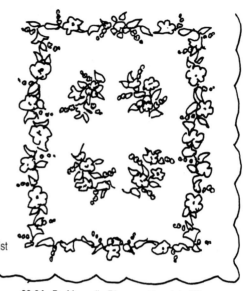

82.84 D Magnolia Blooms—Mountain Mist

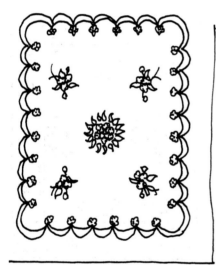

82.85 D Columbine Quilt—*Needlecraft Magazine*
Columbine Special—Rainbow #328

82.86 D A Beautiful Patchwork Spread—
Home Needlework Magazine

82.87 D The Wild Rose—Boag kit

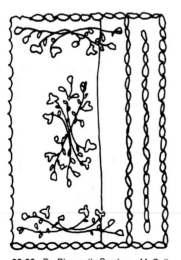

82.88 D Plymouth Garden—*McCalls*

82.89 D Unnamed—Wheeler/Brooks #565

82.91 D The Dolly Varden—Mrs. Danner Books 1 & 2

82.921 D Unknown—Anne Orr #A6601

82.923 D Roosevelt Rose—
Finley in *Good Housekeeping*

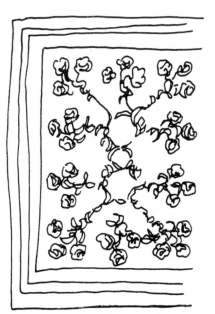

82.93 D American Beauty Climbing Rose—Source not found

82.94 D Wild Rose—Webster

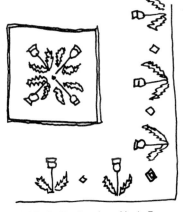

82.95 D Patches for a Man's Room—
Modern Priscilla 1925

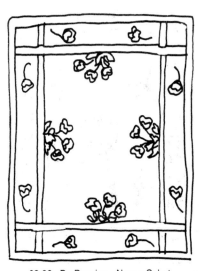

82.96 D Pansies—Nancy Cabot,
Chicago Tribune 1935. See 86.15

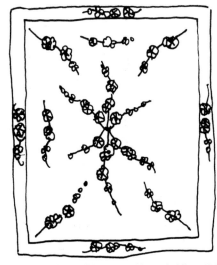

82.973 D Cherry Blossoms—Mountain Mist #104

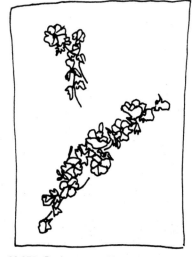

82.975 D Anemone—Mountain Mist #126

82.98 D The Initial Quilt—Anne Orr

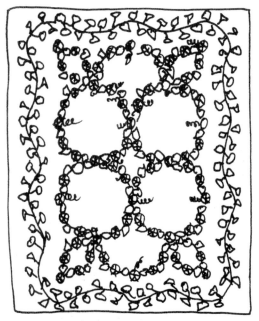

82.992 D Morning Glory—Mountain Mist

82.994 D White Dogwood—Webster in *Ladies Home Journal* 1912 Dogwood Quilt—Webster

82.997 D Dogwood—Mountain Mist

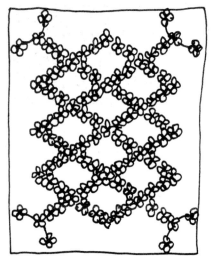

82.998 D Dogwood Beauty—Nancy Cabot, *Chicago Tribune*

Medallions/Fruit 83

83.1 D Orange Blossoms—Mountain Mist

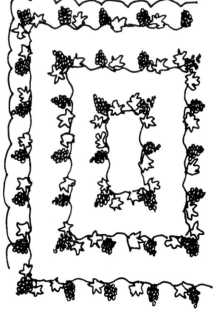

83.22 D Wedgewood—Mrs. Danner

83.23 D Unnamed—from a quilt ca. 1940 in *Quilt Engagement Calendar* 1991, plate 40

84.1 T Unnamed—from a quilt ca. 1890 in Woodard and Greenstein/Crib Quilts. fig. 87

84.2 T Oak Leaves with Cherries—Kimball

84.4 T Unnamed—from a quilt dated 1818 in Spencer Museum

84.6 D Bachelor's Quilt—St. Louis Fancy Work #1216

85.13 D Bambino Spread—
Needlecraft Magazine 1923

85.11 D Little Man in the Moon—Ladies Art Company

85.12 D Crib Blanket—*Needlecraft Magazine* 1926

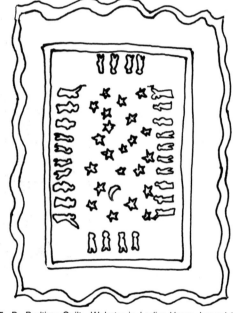

85.15 D Bedtime Quilt—Webster in *Ladies Home Journal* 1912

85.17 D Kiddies' Ride—Needlecraft kit

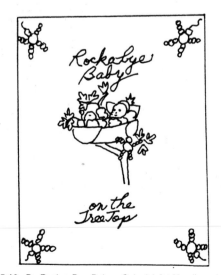

85.18 D Rock-a-Bye Baby—Colonial Art Needlework kit

85.21 D Little Miss Tiptoe—*Needlecraft Magazine*

85.22 D Mistress Betty—*Modern Priscilla* 1922

85.26 D Dutch Girl—Anne Orr in *Good Housekeeping*   **85.27** D Dutch Boy—Anne Orr in *Good Housekeeping*

85.31 D Keepsake Quilt—Webster in *Ladies Home Journal* 1912

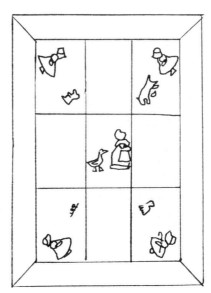

85.33 D Mother Goose—Boag kit

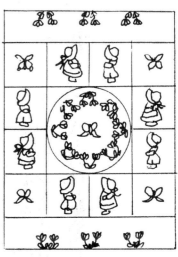

85.35 D Small Fry—Mountain Mist

85.37 D Sun Bonnet Babe—Boag kit

85.42 D Old Woman in the Shoe—*Needlecraft Magazine*

85.44 D Little Red Riding Hood—*Needlecraft Magazine*

85.49 D Cinderella—Needlecraft kit

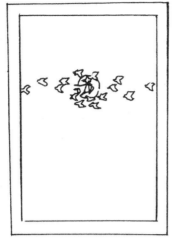

85.5 D Hallo Een Quilt—Nancy Cabot, *Chicago Tribune* 1935

86.13 D Butterflies—Mountain Mist

86.15 D Golden Butterflies and Pansies—Webster. See 82.96

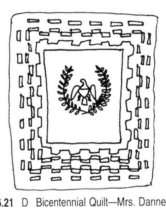

86.21 D Bicentennial Quilt—Mrs. Danner

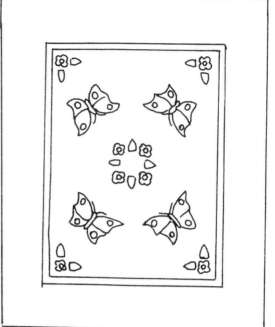

86.23 T Unnamed—one of several similar quilts made in Maryland ca. 1830. Border is reverse applique

86.24 T American Glory—Paragon kit (drawn after quilt ca. 1850)

86.25 T Spread Eagle—*Omaha World Herald* 1912

86.3 T Unnamed—numerous examples ca. 1880,
common in Pennsylvania

86.41 D Unnamed—*McCalls* #2701D

86.42 D Unknown—from a clipping 1916

86.43 D Three Little Kittens—Source not found

86.44 D Unknown—Source not found

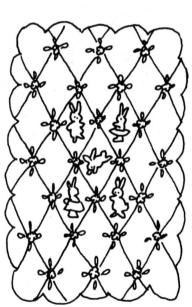

86.52 D Bunnies—Needlecraft kit

86.53 D Bunnies—Mountain Mist

86.54 D Unnamed—Anne Orr

86.55 D Bedtime Bunnies—*Modern Priscilla* kit 1927

86.6 D Unknown—
kit source not found

86.71 D Noah's Ark—source not found

86.72 D Noah's Ark—Designs Worth Doing

86.74 D Unnamed—*McCalls*

86.8 D The Elephant's Child—
E. Buckner Kirk in *Woman's Home Companion* 1934

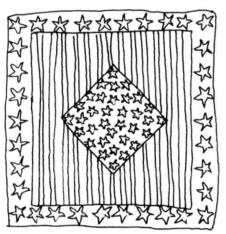

87.1 T A Patriotic Quilt—*Peterson's Magazine* May/June 1861

87.2 T Flag—from a quilt 1932 in Woodard and
Greenstein/*20th Century*, pg. 99

87.33 T Flags and Shields—from a quilt 1921, Kansas Quilt Project

87.35 T Unnamed—from a quilt 1898 in Bishop and Houck

88.12 D Autumn Leaf—Anne Orr 1932

88.14 D Autumn Leaves—Nancy Cabot, *Chicago Tribune* and Sears

88.15 D Tree of Life—McKim

88.17 D Autumn Leaves—Needlecraft Supply Co. kit 1935

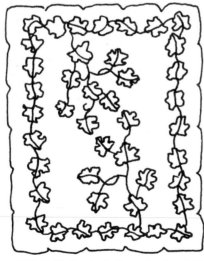

88.2 D Trailing Leaf—Home Needlecraft kit

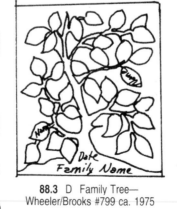

88.3 D Family Tree—
Wheeler/Brooks #799 ca. 1975

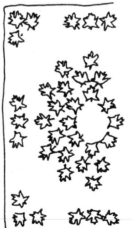

88.4 D North Across the Border—*McCalls*

88.5 D Christmas Tree Quilt—*Needlecraft Magazine* 1924

88.6 D American Heritage—Bucilla kit #1894

88.72 D Rose Tree—Mountain Mist. See 37.246

88.74 D Blossom Time—
Homeneedlecraft Creations #7066

88.8 D Tree of Life—Progress kit #1369

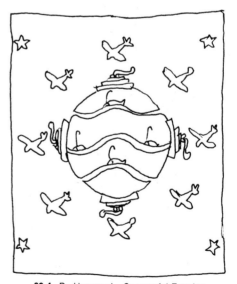

89.4 D Unnamed—*Successful Farming*

89.2 D Early American—Paragon kit

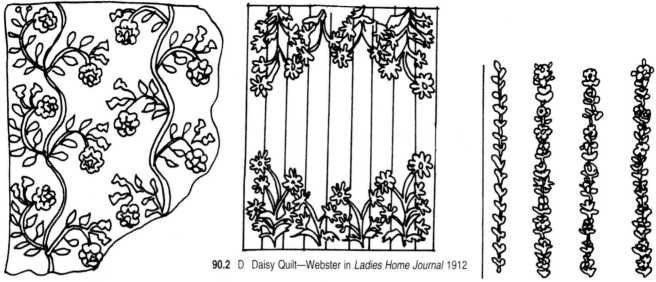

90.1 T Rose of Sharon—from a quilt in Havig/Missouri, pg. 71

90.2 D Daisy Quilt—Webster in *Ladies Home Journal* 1912

90.31 D Magic Vine—Nancy Page 1930

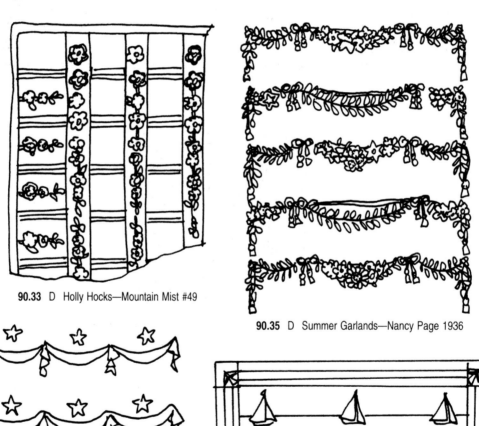

90.33 D Holly Hocks—Mountain Mist #49

90.35 D Summer Garlands—Nancy Page 1936

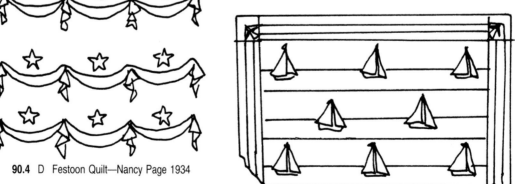

90.4 D Festoon Quilt—Nancy Page 1934

90.5 D Snug Harbor—Anne Orr

91.1 T Rocky Mountain—*Ladies Home Journal* 7/1909
The Great Divide—*Ladies Home Journal* 7/1909
See as a pieced design #1083 and as applique #25.9

91.2 T Unnamed—from a quilt dated 1874

91.3 T Vining New York Beauty—Texas Heritage Quilt Society

Album. Refers to an album, sampler, or friendship quilt, usually with an inscribed date.

Arkansas Quilters Guild. *Arkansas Quilts* (Paducah, KY: American Quilters Society).

Aunt Martha Studios. Booklets, kits, and related items are still offered by Kansas City's Colonial Patterns, Inc., which began in the early 1930s when it advertised in a syndicated column under various names, including Aunt Ellen, Aunt Matilda, Betsy Ross, Royal Neighbor, and Colonial Quilt. Aunt Martha was the most common name used. In 1949, Colonial Patterns and *Workbasket* magazine (see entry) split.

Bishop, Robert. *The Knopf Collector's Guides to American Antiques, Quilts, Coverlets, Rugs & Samplers* (New York: Alfred A. Knopf, 1982).

Bishop, Robert, and Patricia Coblentz. *New Discoveries in American Quilts* (New York: E. P. Dutton, 1975).

Bishop, Robert, and Carter Houck. *All Flags Flying* (New York: E. P. Dutton, 1986).

Boag. Chicago kit company acquired by Collingbourne Mills of Elgin, Illinois, in 1927.

Bresenhan, Karoline Patterson, and Nancy O'Bryant Puentes. *Lone Star: A Legacy of Texas Quilts, 1836–1936* (Austin: University of Texas Press, 1986).

Brooks, Alice. See Wheeler, Laura.

Bucilla. Kit company founded in 1867 in New York, Bucilla is an acronym for Bernhard Ulmann Inc. Lace, Linen and Accessories. Purchased by Indian Head Corp. in 1962, it is now part of the Plaid Creative Group.

Bureau Farmer. Periodical from the American Farm Bureau Federation, 1925–1935.

Cabot, Nancy. Daily quilt column by Loretta Leitner Rising (1906–1958) in the *Chicago Tribune*, beginning in January 1933. The *Tribune* sold hundreds of Cabot pattern sheets by mail and grouped them in booklets through the 1930s and 1940s. *Progressive Farmer* and the Spinning Wheel syndicate sold the same patterns through the 1960s.

Capper's Weekly. Periodical from Topeka's Capper Publications, which was begun in 1904 and is still published as *Capper's Magazine*. From 1927 through 1935, offered a unique column authored by staff member Louise Fowler Roote (1898–1987), writing as Kate Marchbanks, fictitious editor of the women's page, titled "In the Heart of the Home." Since 1935, have offered various syndicated columns, particularly Famous Features (see entry), which incorporated some of Roote's designs. Other Capper publications with quilt patterns: *The Kansas Farmer, Capper's Farmer, Capper's Farm Press, The Mail & Breeze,* and *The Household Magazine.*

Chicago Art Institute. Catalog: Mildred Davison. *American Quilts 1819–1948 from the Museum Collection* (Chicago: The Art Institute of Chicago, 1959).

Clark, Grandmother. Series of booklets from needlework company W.L.M. Clark Inc. of St. Louis. Also sold quilt kits. Occasionally used the name Winifred Clark. The company began publishing quilt patterns in the early 1930s and continued selling stamped needlework items into the 1950s.

Clark, Ricky, George W. Knepper, and Ellice Ronsheim. *Quilts in Community, Ohio's Traditions* (Nashville, TN: Rutledge Hill, 1991).

Clarke, Mary Washington. *Kentucky Quilts and Their Makers* (Lexington: University Press of Kentucky, 1976).

Coats and Clark. Thread manufacturer that published at least two pattern booklets: *Quilts* (1945) and *Heirloom Quilts* (no date).

Comfort. Periodical begun in Augusta, Maine, by William H. Gannet in 1888. Absorbed by *Needlecraft Magazine* in 1940. *Comfort* published patterns, offered them as premiums for subscriptions, and sold patterns and kits by mail. Editors included Mrs. Wheeler Wilkinson and Mollie Millard. Booklet: *Comfort's Appliqué and Patchwork: Revival of Old Time Patchwork* (1921 or 1922).

Country Gentleman. Periodical founded in 1853; changed to *Better Farming* in 1955 and merged with *Farm Journal* that year. Sold mail-order patterns in the 1930s and published articles by Velma Mackey Paul and Florence LaGanke Harris, among others.

Country Home. Periodical that published patterns in the 1930s.

Country Life. Periodical that published patterns at the turn of the twentieth century.

Crews, Patricia Cox, and Ronald C. Naugle (eds.). *Nebraska Quilts* (Lincoln: University of Nebraska Press, 1991).

Danner, Scioto Imhoff. Mrs. Danner's Quilts in El Dorado, Kansas; begun in 1934 by Scioto Danner (1891–1974), who sold mail-order pattern sheets through a series of booklets. Helen Ericson bought the company in 1970. Danner published four pamphlets, and Ericson added four more.

Davis, Carolyn O'Bagy. *Pioneer Quiltmaker: The Story of Dorinda Moody Slade* (Tucson, AZ: Sanpete Publications, 1990).

Denver Art Museum. Catalogs: Lydia Roberts Dunham, *Denver Art Museum Quilt Collection* (no date). Imelda DeGraw, *Quilts and Coverlets*, 1974.

Dexter, Grandma. Series of booklets published in the early 1930s from the Virginia Snow Studios, part of the Dexter Yarn and Thread Company and the Collingbourne Mills in Elgin, Illinois. Some syndicated column advertisements appeared in newspapers.

Family, The. An undocumented magazine. I have a 1913 clipping with several appliqué patterns.

Famous Features. Syndicated mail-order source that still sells pattern booklets. Some pattern collectors call them the Q Books, because each number is preceded by a Q. These booklets appear

to have begun in the 1940s, probably an outgrowth of *Capper's Weekly* patterns (see entry). Authors include Mabel Obenchain and Louise Fowler Roote.

Farm and Fireside. Periodical begun in Springfield, Ohio, in 1878 by Crowell, which also published *Household Journal* (see entry). Renamed *Country Home* in 1930 and ceased in 1939. Quilt patterns begun in 1884 may be the earliest regularly appearing quilt feature.

Farm and Home. Periodical that printed patterns after the mid-1880s.

Farm Journal. Periodical begun in 1877 and still publishing. Has absorbed at least three other pattern sources (*Country Gentleman*, *The Farmer's Wife*, and *Household Journal*). In the twentieth century, offered mail-order patterns and booklets.

Farmer's Wife, The. Periodical published in St. Paul from the nineteenth century through 1939, when it merged with *Farm Journal*. In the 1930s, sold three booklets edited by Lorene Dunnigan, Orrine Johnson, and Eleanor C. Lewis.

Finley, Ruth. *Old Patchwork Quilts and the Women Who Made Them* (Philadelphia: J. B. Lippincott, 1929). Reprinted by EPM Publications, McLean, Virginia, 1992.

Fox, Sandi. *Quilts in Utah* (Salt Lake City, UT: Salt Lake Arts Center, 1981).

Fox, Sandi. *Small Endearments* (New York: Charles Scribner's Sons, 1985).

Frank, Robert. Robert Frank Needlework Supply Company of Kalamazoo published at least one booklet: *E-Z Patterns for Patchwork and Appliqué Quilts.*

Gold-Art Needlework. A company producing kits in the mid-twentieth century.

Good Housekeeping. Magazine founded in 1885; acquired by Hearst Corporation in 1911. Anne Orr (see entry) was needlework editor from 1921 to 1939.

Gutcheon, Beth. *The Perfect Patchwork Primer* (New York: David McKay, 1973).

Hagerman, Betty J. *A Meeting of the Sunbonnet Children* (Baldwin, KS: Author, 1979).

Hall, Carrie A., and Rose G. Kretsinger. *The Romance of the Patchwork Quilt in America* (Caldwell, ID: Caxton Printers, 1935).

Havig, Bettina. *Missouri Heritage Quilts* (Paducah, KY: American Quilter's Society, 1986).

Hearth and Home. Periodical from Vickery and Hill (see entry) of Augusta, Maine, 1885–1933. Printed numerous patterns and sold sheets by mail after 1895.

Herrschner, Frederick. Herrschner began a Chicago pattern company in 1899 that has designed and retailed patterns by others in mail-order catalogs into the twenty-first century.

Hinson, Delores A. *Quilting Manual* (New York: Hearthside Press, 1966).

Hinson, Delores A. *A Quilter's Companion* (New York: Arco, 1973).

Holstein, Jonathan, and John Finley. *Kentucky Quilts: 1800–1900* (Louisville: Kentucky Quilt Project, 1982).

Homeneedlecraft Creations. Kit company.

Horton, Laurel. *Social Fabric: South Carolina's Traditional Quilts* (Columbia: McKissick Museum, University of South Carolina, 1984).

Household, The. See *Capper's Weekly.*

Household Journal. Periodical published in Springfield, Ohio, in the early twentieth century by Crowell, which also published *Farm and Fireside.* Moved to Batavia, Illinois, and changed to *Household Management Journal.* Later absorbed by *Farm Journal.* Sold patterns under the name Aunt Jane. Booklets: *Aunt Jane's Quilt Pattern Book* (no date); *Aunt Jane's Prize Winning Quilt Designs* (1914).

Ickis, Marguerite. *The Standard Book of Quilt Making and Collecting* (Greystone Press, New York, 1949). Reprinted by Dover Publications, New York, NY, 1959.

Indiana Quilt Registry Project. *Quilts of Indiana* (Bloomington: Indiana University Press, 1991).

Kansas City Star. Patterns appeared in three periodicals (*Kansas City Star, Weekly Kansas City Star,* and *Weekly Star Farmer*) from 1928 to 1960. Early patterns were McKim syndicated patterns (see entry). After 1929, a unique quilt column edited first by Eveline Foland (1893–?) and later by Edna Marie Dunn (1893–1983) ran weekly. In 2001, a block of the month pattern began in the Sunday *Star Magazine* insert.

Kimball, Jeana. *Red and Green: An Appliqué Tradition* (Bothell, WA: That Patchwork Place, 1990).

Ladies Art Company (LAC). Founded in St. Louis in 1889 by Henry M. Brockstedt, who is credited with the first mail-order quilt pattern catalog, *Diagrams of Quilt,*

Sofa and Pin Cushion Patterns. An 1895 ad mentions 272 patterns. The 1906 edition included 450 designs. A second catalog, *Quilt Patterns: Patchwork and Appliqué,* was published in 1922 and revised again between 1928 and 1934, with patterns through 531. This last catalog was published until the company went out of business in the 1970s. Pattern historians Cuesta Benberry and Wilene Smith noted that a pattern's number can be used to date it (with exceptions). Appliqué designs from the 1920s were usually numbered in four digits. Following is an index to dates and three-digit numbers drawn from Smith's research, "Quilt History in Old Periodicals: A New Interpretation," in *Uncoverings 1990,* Laurel Horton, ed. (San Francisco: The American Quilt Study Group, 1991).

LAC Patterns numbered 1–272 published 1889; 273–400 published 1897; 401–420 published 1901; 421–450 published 1906; 451–500 published 1922; 501–509 published 1928; 511–530 published 1934; and 531 published 1934.

Ladies Home Journal. Periodical begun as *Ladies' Journal and Practical Housekeeper* in 1883. Has published patterns until the present. Marie Webster contributed a number of patterns in the first quarter of the twentieth century.

Lady's Circle Patchwork Quilts. Periodical published by Lopez Publications from 1973 to 1998. Editors: Carter Houck, Karen O'Dowd.

Lasansky, Jeannette. *In the Heart of Pennsylvania: 19th and 20th Century Quiltmaking Traditions* (Lewisburg, PA: Oral Traditions Project, 1985).

Lasansky, Jeannette. *Pieced by Mother: Over 100 Years of Quiltmaking Tradition* (Lewisburg, PA: Oral Traditions Project, 1987).

Lockport Batting Company, Lockport, New York. In addition to selling supplies, the company sold patterns from the 1930s through the 1950s, some by Anne Orr and Mary McElwain (see entries). Booklets: *Replicas of Famous Quilts, Old and New* (1942); *The Lockport Quilt Pattern Book* (no date). Lockport bought Rock River Cotton in 1952.

MacDowell, Marsha, and Ruth D. Fitzgerald. *Michigan Quilts: 150 Years of a Textile Tradition* (East Lansing: Michigan State Museum, 1987).

Marston, Gwen, and Joe Cunningham. *American Beauties: Rose and Tulip Quilts* (Paducah, KY: American Quilter's Society, 1988).

McCall's Needlework. James McCall began a fashion periodical called *The Queen* in 1870, changed to *McCall's Magazine: The Queen of Fashion* in 1889. The publishers offered quilt patterns through *McCall's Magazine* (ceased 2001) and *McCall's Needlework* (ceased in the 1990s). McCall's Patterns continues to sell packaged fashion patterns.

McElwain, Mary A. The Mary McElwain Quilt Shop in Walworth, Wisconsin, sold mail-order patterns, kits, finished quilts, and basted tops. McElwain (1869–1943) opened the shop in 1912. Some were included as premiums in batting from Lockport and Rock River Cotton. Booklet: *The Romance of Village Quilts* (1936; later reprinted by Rock River Cotton, Janesville, Wisonsin, ca. 1955).

McKim, Ruby. *Ruby Short McKim* (1891–1976) syndicated an embroidered quilt pattern in 1916 (possibly the first syndicated quilt pattern). She established McKim Studios in Independence, Missouri, in the early 1920s, selling needlework patterns and kits. In 1928, she began a weekly quilt pattern column for the *Kansas City Star* (see entry), which was syndicated to numerous periodicals and collected in 1931 into a book *101 Patchwork Patterns*. She also wrote for *Better Homes & Gardens*, *Child Life*, and *Successful Farming*.

Meeker, L. K. *Quilt Patterns for the Collector* (Portland, OR: Author, 1979).

Modern Priscilla. Periodical begun in Boston in 1887 that offered mail-order patterns, 1910–1930. Absorbed by *Needlecraft/The Home Arts Magazine* (see entry) in 1930. Booklet: *Priscilla Patchwork Book #1*, 1925.

Mountain Mist. In 1928, Stearns & Foster of Cincinnati began packing Mountain Mist batting in a paper wrapper printed with full-sized quilt patterns. In 1930, they began selling mail-order patterns. Merikay Waldvogel has indexed more than 100 patterns, many of which are still available. The company quilt persona is named Phoebe Edwards.

Needlecraft Magazine. Periodical begun by Vickery and Hill Publishing in Augusta, Maine, in 1909. The name changed several times over the years to *Needlecraft/ The Home Arts Magazine* and *Homes Arts/Needlecraft*. It absorbed *Modern Priscilla* in 1930 and ceased publication in 1943. (See *Hearth & Home*.)

Oklahoma Farmer Stockman. Periodical published in Oklahoma City. In about 1930, it carried a unique column titled "Good Cheer Quilt Patterns."

Orlofsky, Myron, and Patsy Orlofsky. *Quilts in America* (New York: McGraw Hill, 1974). Reprinted by Abbeville Press, New York, 1992.

Orr, Anne. Designer of quilt and other needlework patterns in the early twentieth century and a needlework editor at *Good Housekeeping Magazine* from 1921 to 1939. Anne Orr (ca. 1869–1946) sold patterns under her name, along with *Good Housekeeping* and the Lockport Batting Company (see entries).

Page, Nancy. A mail-order column written by food writer Florence LaGanke Harris (1886–1972), syndicated in many periodicals from 1928 to 1938. She specialized in appliquéd series designs.

Paragon. Paragon Needlecraft sold kits in the last half of the twentieth century through magazines, including *Woman's Day*, and in catalogs, such as Herrschner's.

Penny, Prudence. Food writer Bernice Redington (1892–1966) edited a unique quilt column for the *Seattle Post-Intelligencer* in the 1920s and 1930s. It was syndicated to a few other papers. Booklet: *Old Time Quilts*, 1927.

People's Popular Monthly. A periodical published from 1896 to 1931, which absorbed *Ladies' Favorite Magazine* in 1908.

Peterson's Magazine. A periodical begun in 1842 as *Lady's World of Fashion*. The owners changed the name in 1849 and merged with *Argosy* in 1894. Occasionally showed quilt patterns.

Peto, Florence. *Historic Quilts* (New York: American Historical, 1939).

Peto, Florence. *American Quilts and Coverlets* (New York: Chanticleer Press, 1949).

Progress. A kit company that marketed through magazines and catalogs in the last half of the twentieth century.

Quilt Engagement Calendar. Annual desk calendar edited by Cyril Nelson (1927–2005), published by E. P. Dutton from 1975 to 2001. See a selection in Cyril I. Nelson and Carter Houck, *The Quilt Engagement Treasury* (New York: E. P. Dutton, 1982).

Quilters Newsletter Magazine. Periodical published since 1969, founded by Bonnie Leman.

Rainbow. The Rainbow Quilt Block Company, which was begun in the 1920s by William Pinch (1880–1972) in Cleveland, was best known for stamped blocks for embroidery. Also sold appliqué kits in block form. Most of the patterns indexed here are appliqué combined with embroidery.

Ramsey, Bets, and Merikay Waldvogel. *Quilts of Tennessee: Images of Domestic Life Prior to 1930* (Nashville, TN: Rutledge Hill Press, 1986).

Roan, Nancy. *Just A Quilt/ Juscht En Deppich* (Green Lane, PA: Goschenhoppen Historians, 1984).

Roberson, Ruth Haslip ed. *North Carolina Quilts* (Chapel Hill: University of North Carolina Press, 1988).

Rural New Yorker. Periodical begun in 1841 and published through the mid-twentieth century. Mrs. R. E. Smith edited a unique pattern column from 1930 through 1937. She mentioned the column was syndicated, but I have not seen it elsewhere.

Safford, Carleton L., and Robert Bishop. *America's Quilts and Coverlets* (New York: E. P. Dutton, 1972).

St. Louis Fancywork Company. An art needlework company that sold quilt patterns as Martha Washington Patchwork. Designers were Amy Conway and Sophie T. LaCroix. Booklet: *Martha Washington Patchwork*, 1916.

Sears, Roebuck & Co. *Century of Progress in Quilt Making.* (Chicago: Author, 1934). Booklet featuring winners of the company's contest held in conjunction with the 1933 World's Fair.

Sexton, Carlie. Carlie Sexton Holmes (1877–1964) ran a mail-order pattern company from Wheaton, Illinois, in the 1920s and 1930s. Susan Price Miller attributes unsigned quilt articles for *People's Popular Monthly* in the teens to Sexton and notes her first byline in 1920, suggesting readers write Sexton for patterns. Also wrote for Meredith Corporation, publisher of *Successful Farming* and *Better Homes & Gardens.* Booklets: *Old Fashioned Quilts* (1928); *Yesterday's Quilts in Homes of Today* (1928); *How to Make a Quilt* (1932).

Shelburne Museum, Shelburne, Vermont. Catalogs indexed here: Lillian Baker Carlisle, *Pieced Work and Appliqué Quilts at Shelburne Museum* (1957); Celia Y. Oliver, *55 Famous Quilts from the Shelburne Museum* (1991).

Sienkiewicz, Elly. *Spoken Without a Word, A Lexicon of Symbols with Twenty-Four Patterns from the Baltimore Album Quilts* (Washington, DC: Author, 1983).

Sienkiewicz, Elly. *Baltimore Beauties and Beyond, Studies in Classic Album Quilt Appliqué,* Vol. I and II (Lafayette, CA: C & T Publishing, 1989 and 1990).

Spencer Museum of Art, University of Kansas. Catalogs: *One Hundred Years of American Quilts* (1973); *Quilters Choice* (1978); *American Patchwork Quilt* (1988).

Successful Farming. Periodical published by Meredith Corporation, Des Moines, Iowa; begun in 1902 and still publishing. See Carlie Sexton.

Texas Heritage Quilt Society. *Texas Quilts, Texas Treasures* (Paducah, KY: American Quilter's Society, 1986).

Uncoverings. The annual papers of the American Quilt Study Group, published since 1980.

Vickery Publishing. Company also known as Vickery and Hill from Augusta, Maine. Published numerous magazines with quilt patterns in the early twentieth century: *American Woman, Fireside Visitor, Good Stories, Happy Hours, Hearth & Home,* and *Needlecraft.*

Webster, Marie D. *Quilts: Their Story and How to Make Them* (New York: Tudor Publishing, 1915). Webster designed quilt patterns for the *Ladies Home Journal* and sold mail-order patterns from her home in Marion, Indiana.

Wheeler, Laura, or Alice Brooks. Names used by Needlecraft Service, a mail-order company begun in 1933 that continues to advertise in periodicals, although most of their quilt patterns are no longer offered. Other names include Carol Curtis and Reader Mail. Patterns were sold in the sheet or in booklets.

Wilkinson Art Quilts. Company founded by the Wilkinson sisters, Iona and Rosalie, in 1914 in Ligonier, Indiana. Sold finished quilts, primarily wholecloth, from their own patterns until the studio closed in 1943.

Woman's Day. Periodical that has included quilt patterns from the 1940s to the present. Some articles were reprinted in Rose Wilder Lane's *Woman's Day Book of American Needlework* (New York: Simon & Schuster, 1962).

Woman's Home Companion. Periodical begun toward the end of the nineteenth century in Cleveland. Occasionally published quilt patterns. Ceased in 1957.

Woman's World. Periodical published by the Manning Publishing Company, Chicago, in the 1920s and 1930s. The current *Woman's World* is unrelated. Booklet: *The Patchwork Book* (1931).

Woodard, Thomas K., and Blanche Greenstein. *Crib Quilts and Other Small Wonders* (New York: E. P. Dutton, 1981).

Woodard, Thomas K., and Blanche Greenstein. *Twentieth Century Quilts 1900–1950* (New York: E. P. Dutton, 1988).

Workbasket, The. Periodical begun in 1935 as a leaflet by Colonial Patterns. Affiliated with the Aunt Martha Studios (see entry) until 1949, when Modern Handcrafts began publishing *The Workbasket.* After 1950, the magazine rarely published quilt patterns and ceased publication in 1996.

ALPHABETICAL INDEX *to* NAMES

Canada Lily, 33.43

Cape Cod Basket, 80.41

Cape Cod Quilt, 82.17

Cardinal & Morning Glory, 52.44

Cardinal Climber, 35.24

Carlie Sexton's Basket, 42.715

Carnation, 82.74

Carolina Medallion, 15.93

Cathedral Bells, 32.82

Centennial, 60.42

Centennial Wreath, 2.73

Chanticleer, 53.18

Charming Nosegay, 39.13

Charter Oak, 5.71, 10.67

Cherries, 43.54

Cherry, 13.14, 26.92

Cherry Blossoms, 82.973

Cherry Trees, 57.6

Cherry Wreaths, 1.34

Chestnut Berry, 16.65

Chick in Boots, 53.22

Children's Nursery Blocks, 74.13

China Aster, 27.15

Christmas Rose, 36.63

Christmas Toy Quilt, 75.59

Christmas Tree Quilt, 88.5

Chrysanthemum, 5.76, 27.12, 33.62, 33.63

Cinderella, 85.49

Circle of Godetias, 36.55

Clematis, 21.44

Cleome, 22.74

Climbing Rose, 82.13, 82.51

Cliveden Quilt, 33.83

Clover Block, 20.26

Cluster of Roses, 2.51, 82.82

Cochise County, 19.31

Cock's Comb, 18.11, 19.83

Cockscomb, 19.38, 23.3, 41.46, 43.72
  (see Coxcomb)

Cockscombs & Currants, 16.68

Colonial Belle, 74.25

Colonial Ladies, 47.58

Colonial Lady, 47.9, 74.21

Colonial Patchwork, 8.58

Colonial Rose, 11.42, 11.42b, 11.55

Colonial Tulip, 28.18

Columbine, 34.16, 82.85

Columbine Special, 82.85

Combination Rose, 11.831, 18.22

Compass, 17.11

Coneflower, 10.61

Conventional Appliqué, 19.58

Conventional Fleur-de-lis, 37.78

Conventional Flower, 37.913, 81.76

Conventional Lily Appliqué, 12.63

Conventional Rose, 14.74

Conventional Rose Wreath, 2.31

Conventional Scroll, 45.42

Conventional Tulip, 5.42, 29.42, 29.48, 29.89, 44.4, 45.19

Conventional Tulips, 8.56, 25.26

Conventional Wild Rose, 11.21

Cornflower, 36.59

Corsage Bouquet, 34.42

Cosmos, 20.32

Cottage Behind the Hill, 58.18

Cotton Boll, 5.76, 9.68, 29.7

Coverlet in Floral Design, 72.3

Cowboy, 49.13, 49.17

Cowboy & Horse, 49.15, 49.16, 49.18

Cowgirl, 49.12

Coxcomb, 9.43, 19.75, 22.72, 41.12, 41.42, 41.44, 41.48, 43.76
  (see Cockscomb)

Coxcomb & Currants, 16.63

Coxcombs & Currants, 16.62

Creation of the Animals, 50.4

Crescent Moon, 60.78

Crib Blanket, 85.12

Crib Cover, 75.23

Crib Quilt, 81.1

Crib Quilt of Sleepy Time Pets, 75.24

Crocus Wreath, 3.94

Crossed Laurel Spray, 21.28

Crown of Oaks, 17.23

Cucumber, 15.7

Cupid's Block, 36.56

Curious Chicks, 52.24

Curling Leaves, 9.41

Currants & Cockscombs, 16.61

Cut Tulips, 39.48

Cyclamen, 12.47

Daffodil, 39.7

Daffodils, 37.82, 37.84

Daffodils & Butterflies, 26.65

Dahlia, 10.85, 37.211

Dahlia Flowerpot, 39.59

Dahlia Wreath, 2.34, 3.31, 3.34

Dainty Block, 36.11

Daisy, 10.35, 26.51, 26.52

Daisy Chain, 81.5

Daisy Quilt, 90.2

Damask Rose, 34.29

Dancing Daffodil, 26.64, 37.89

Dancing Jumbo, 56.46

Decorated Basket, 42.713

Decorative Flowers, 32.74

Decorative Plant, 41.93

Delphinium, 21.32

Delphiniums, 33.81

Democrat Rose, 18.24, 18.35, 20.92

Democratic Rose, 12.84, 18.5, 41.99

Desert Bell Flower, 32.93

Des Moines Rose, 3.7

Diamond Vine, 20.97

Dianthus, 36.58

Dickey Bird, 52.3

Dicky, 49.86

Dixie Rose, 33.32

Dog Appliqué, 55.55

Doggie Appliqué, 55.54

Dogwood, 9.912, 21.14, 22.34, 32.11, 32.13, 34.75, 82.994, 82.997

Dogwood Basket, 80.13

Dogwood Beauty, 82.998

Dolly Varden, 82.91

Dotty, 49.85

Double Dahlia, 14.26, 20.22

Double Heart, 9.843

Double Hearts, 14.95, 24.4

Double Irish Cross, 9.812

Double Peony & Wild Rose, 12.93

Double Poppy, 9.921, 27.81

Double Tulip, 12.93, 37.12

Dove Appliqué, 52.12

Dream Ship, 59.24

Dresden Plate, 27.3

Ducky Coverlet, 53.35

Ducky Doo, 53.44

Dutch Boy, 48.17, 49.63, 85.27

Dutch Boy & Girl, 49.68

Dutch Girl, 47.48, 85.26

Dutch Girls, 49.62

Dutch Lass, 49.61

Dutch Roses, 39.25

Dutch Tulip, 8.33, 28.13

Dutch Tulip Basket, 42.77

Dutch Tulips, 29.52

Eagle Appliqué, 54.7

Early American, 89.2

Early Rose of Sharon, 31.82

Early to Bed, 49.78

Early Tulips, 29.964, 29.99

Easter Lilies, 22.85

Eastern Star, 60.71

Edith Hall's Rose, 13.43

Egyptian Lotus, 42.93

Egyptian Lotus Flower, 41.56

Eight of Hearts, 9.842

Eight Pointed Star with Sprigs, 14.83

Elderberry Bloom, 12.37

Elephant, 56.42, 56.45, 56.47

Elephant's Child, 86.8

Emporia Rose, 36.25

Enchanted Cottage, 58.16

English Flower Garden, 39.24

English Garden, 39.24

English Rose, 12.88

Esther's Plume, 36.73
Evening Flower Block, 32.52
Evergreen Tree, 57.7
Falling Leaves, 71.3
Family Tree, 88.3
Fancy Butterfly, 51.14
Farmer Boy, 48.24, 48.7
Farmer's Barometer, 25.3
Feather, 19.62
Feather Crown, 1.13
Feather Crown with Ragged Robin, 1.13
Feather Flower, 37.99
Feather Rose, 15.22, 36.75
Festoon Quilt, 90.4
Field Daisy, 26.53
Field Flowers, 33.59, 37.59
Firefly, 51.4
Fireworks, 10.89
First Lady, 81.63
Fisher Boy, 48.54
Fisher Lad, 48.52
Five Roses, 20.8
Flag, 87.2
Flags, 37.7
Flags & Shields, 87.33
Flame Block, 5.74
Flames, 5.74
Flamingoes, 53.6
Flanders Poppy, 37.52
Flemish Tile, 9.924
Fleur-de-lis, 6.6
Fleur-de-lis with Folded Rose Buds, 3.84
Floral, 9.59
Floral Basket, 80.12
Floral Block, 10.13
Floral Wreath, 21.94
Flower Basket, 41.16, 42.66, 42.715,
    42.732, 42.735, 42.742, 73.2
Flower Bowl, 73.3
Flowered Cross, 20.8
Flower Garden, 72.2, 72.9, 80.11
Flower Girl, 47.33
Flowering Almond, 16.65
Flowering Balsam, 37.17
Flowering Fan, 19.43
Flower of Spring, 37.35, 41.13
Flower Pot Combination, 73.5
Flowers in a Pot, 40.13
Flower Spears, 33.47
Flower Spray, 35.31
Flower Tree, 33.46
Flower Urn, 40.5, 41.54
Flower Wreath, 2.24, 4.92
Flying Bird, 52.14
Foliage Wreath, 1.26
Forest, 19.24

Forest Bouquet, 20.35
Forest Bride's Quilt, 57.1
Forget-Me-Not, 9.912, 12.41, 22.45,
    34.57, 35.12
Formal Garden, 82.25
Fortune's Wheel, 27.7
Foundation Rose & Pine Tree, 13.13
Four Baskets, 80.48
Four Chartres Lilies, 9.941
Four Flowers Set, 72.1
Four Frogs, 6.3
Four Leaf Clover, 9.821, 43.14
Four Little Birds, 5.8, 41.552
Four Lotus Blossoms, 22.83
Four Poppies & Butterflies, 51.68
Four Square Rose, 37.294
Fourth of July, 60.85
Four Tulips, 8.16, 8.43, 25.24
Fragrance, 42.37
Fredonia Oak Leaf, 17.22
French Basket, 42.752, 80.43
French Bouquet, 72.4
French Provincial, 42.54
French Rose, 10.24, 36.82
Friendship, 14.16
Friendship Band, 9.913
Friendship Dahlia, 37.915
Friendship Plume, 6.8
Friendship Quilt, 9.843, 9.874
Friendship Ring, 27.12
Fringed Rose, 10.43
Fringed Tulips, 25.5
Frisky Dog, 55.35
Fruit Basket Quilt, 73.6
Fruit Bowl, 42.95
Fuchsia, 21.34, 33.48
Full Blown Rose, 20.24, 20.38
Garden, 82.79
Garden Bounty, 38.34
Garden Bouquet, 42.35, 73.12
Garden Fruits, 73.84
Garden Gift, 42.78
Garden of Eden, 46.12
Garden of Light, 25.27
Garden Paths, 26.47
Garden Wreath, 2.32, 2.62
Garland & Basket, 80.47
Garland of Leaves, 1.64
Gay Butterflies, 51.35
Gay Garden, 45.82
Gay Print Pansy, 37.65
Gay Tulips, 8.56
Geneva Tassel Flower, 9.945
Geometrical Rose, 36.38
Geranium, 39.34
Geranium Wreath, 12.35

Giant Morning Glory, 37.42
Giant Primrose, 34.68
Gift of Love, 60.56
Gingham Bush, 39.9
Gladiola, 82.73
Globe Thistle, 32.57
Golden Bells, 8.92
Golden Butterflies & Pansies, 86.15
Golden Corn, 9.73
Golden Lily, 35.23
Golden Poppies, 42.85
Goldenrod, 21.26
Golden Rose of Virginia, 31.1
Good Luck Block, 9.821
Good Luck Clover, 9.1, 9.822
Gorgeous Pansies, 37.664
Grandmother's Dream, 9.32
Grandmother's Engagement Ring, 25.9
Grandmother's Flower Quilt, 29.26
Grandmother's Garden, 73.7
Grandmother's Prize Quilt, 39.55
Grandmother's Quilt, 11.832
Grandmother's Sunbonnet, 27.12
Grandmother's Sunburst, 27.12
Grape & Morning Glory, 16.3
Grapes, 1.57, 46.83
Grapes & Oak Leaf, 16.67
Grapes & Vines, 26.94
Grapevine Block, 9.63
Grape Wreath, 2.13
Great Divide, 91.1
Hallo E'en Quilt, 85.5
Hallowe'en Block, 50.8
Happy Jack, 48.6
Harebells, 8.87
Harrison Rose, 17.32, 31.25, 31.26
Harvest Rose, 18.74
Hawaiian Blocks, 9.76
Hawaiian Flower, 4.1
Hawthorne Berries, 16.1
Heart & Dove, 52.92
Heart & Spade, 52.92
Heart for Appliqué, 9.874
Hearts, 9.825, 11.12, 24.5
Hearts All Around, 9.85
Hearts & Diamonds, 24.82, 24.86
Hearts & Flowers, 11.23, 21.72, 26.86,
    42.995, 72.6
Heirloom Historic Quilt, 33.18
Hero's Crown, 17.21
Hibiscus, 35.25, 35.27
Hickory Leaf, 17.11, 17.13
Hobby Horse, 56.58
Holland Tulip, 21.56
Hollyhock, 33.56, 35.46
Holly Hocks, 90.33

Sweetheart Quilt, 9.875
Sweetheart Rose, 39.57
Sweethearts, 9.842
Sweet Pea, 45.32
Sweet Peas, 9.45, 22.52
Sweet Pea Wreath, 2.18
Sweet William, 36.53
Swiss Basket, 42.694
Swordbush, 21.66
Tallulah Rose, 36.86
Tangerine, 16.2
Tassel Flower, 22.64
Tea Rose, 18.33, 18.37, 18.6
Teddy Bear, 56.2, 56.23, 56.26, 75.4
Temperance Ball, 46.72
Tennessee Tulip, 8.54
Texas Republic, 34.33
Texas Sunflower, 10.39
Texas Yellow Rose, 11.831
Thistle, 9.47, 12.59
Thistle Block, 9.47
Thistles, 9.48
Three Little Kittens, 75.15, 86.43
Three Little Pigs, 75.3
Three Tulips, 29.94
Tiger Lily, 28.53, 29.24, 29.46, 29.87,
   37.78, 82.72
Tiger Lily & Bud, 33.22
Tile Flower, 41.2
Tipperary Tangle, 9.96
Tobacco Leaf, 5.16
Tobacco Leaves, 5.24
Tomato Flower, 16.7
Topeka Rose, 11.22
Toy Shop Window, 75.52
Toy Soldiers, 49.64
Traditional Geometric Design, 9.844
Trailing Leaf, 88.2
Trailing Vines, 43.33
Treasure Ship, 59.25
Tree of Life, 16.5, 32.91, 37.13, 43.82,
   57.5, 88.15, 88.8
Trees & Garlands, 57.4
Triple Tulip, 29.62
True Lover's Knot, 17.18, 43.43, 45.42
Trumpet Vine, 9.54, 25.12
Tulip, 8.38, 8.64, 8.67, 19.52, 20.44, 20.66,
   21.74, 22.51, 26.34, 26.36, 28.12, 28.16,
   28.19, 28.33, 28.37, 28.42, 28.54, 29.12,
   29.14, 29.53, 29.62, 29.92, 29.95, 29.97,
   30.17, 33.37, 40.63, 42.1, 43.83, 44.2
Tulip & Sun, 28.34
Tulip Basket, 42.58
Tulip Bowl, 40.7
Tulip Circle, 3.92, 21.82
Tulip Crib Quilt, 8.65

Tulip Cross, 19.35, 21.54
Tulip Garden, 28.66, 42.992, 42.993, 45.18
Tulip in a Pot, 39.48
Tulip Pattern, 14.73, 29.35
Tulip Plant, 29.91
Tulip Pot, 40.24
Tulip Quilt, 21.54
Tulips, 28.62, 29.18, 29.22, 29.93,
   29.962, 29.98
Tulips & Buds, 11.95
Tulip Square, 5.94, 26.32
Tulip Swirl, 25.21
Tulip Time, 4.21
Tulip Tree, 44.3
Tulip Tree Leaves, 8.22, 8.24
Tulip Wheel, 36.22
Tulip Wreath, 14.52, 21.82, 81.76
Turkey & Pumpkin, 53.8
Turkey Tracks, 5.36
Turquoise Berries, 9.62
Two Doves, 52.82
$200,000 Tulip, 8.94
United Hearts, 14.97
Urn, 41.72
Valentine, 24.1, 60.53
Valentines, 60.59
Vase of Posies, 42.96
Vase of Roses & Cherries, 1.4
Vases of Roses, 41.97, 42.97
Verbena, 25.4, 34.67
Victorian Rose, 4.72
Victory Garden, 46.24
Victory Quilt, 72.84
Vining New York Beauty, 91.3
Violet Wreath, 36.52
Virginia Rose, 31.54
Virginia Stock, 21.42, 24.3
Viscaria, 34.12
Wandering Foot, 5.36
Washington Feather, 15.14
Washington Square, 6.4
Water Lilies, 26.66, 37.311, 37.32
Water Lily, 37.33, 37.34, 37.372, 37.373
Water Lily Circle, 37.38
Watermelon, 13.31, 26.82
Wax Flowers, 42.997
Wayside Roses, 33.85
Weathervane, 9.926
Wedgewood, 83.22
Whig Rose, 9.99, 14.61, 14.62, 14.63, 14.64,
   14.67, 18.35, 18.79, 18.92, 33.21, 33.24
Whirling Swastika, 10.76
White Day Lily, 29.85
White Dogwood, 82.994
White House Quilt, 82.17
Wild Cherries, 46.89

Wild Ducks, 53.38
Wild Flower, 33.41
Wild Grape, 46.86
Wild Rose, 10.14, 10.52, 11.21, 26.44,
   26.45, 32.14, 34.47, 34.54, 34.65, 34.72,
   35.37, 36.35, 42.634, 82.87, 82.94
Wild Rose of the Andes, 35.36
Wild Rose Bouquet, 35.43
Wild Rose #3, 34.64
Wild Rose Quilt, 10.14
Wild Roses & Squares, 9.97
Wild Rose Spray, 34.46
Wild Rose Wreath, 2.78, 4.4, 4.94
Wild West Quilt, 49.24
Wildwood Wreath, 34.74
Willow Squares, 36.12
Winchester, 6.5
Wind Blown Rose, 36.85
Windblown Daisy, 14.21
Windblown Tulip, 14.54
Winter Garden, 26.24
Wirehaired Pup, 55.43
Wisconsin Rose, 35.45
Wise Old Owl, 52.74
Wisteria, 32.87
Woodland Bells, 32.63
Wreath, 3.1, 73.9
Wreath & Star, 81.94
Wreath of Carnations, 3.32
Wreath of Cherries, 1.33, 1.35
Wreath of Daisies, 4.96
Wreath of Grapes, 1.51
Wreath of Leaves, 1.21
Wreath of Morning Glories, 4.53
Wreath of Pansies, 3.64
Wreath of Roses, 2.16, 2.31, 2.36, 2.4,
   2.55, 2.57, 2.61, 2.62, 2.75, 3.33, 3.36,
   4.78, 81.92
Wreath of Strawberry Leaves, 1.27
Wreath of Violets, 36.52
Wreath of Wild Roses, 3.5
Yellow Hemstitch, 14.24
Yellow Indiana Rose, 12.62
Yellow Iris, 40.35
Yellow Lily Block, 21.84
Yellow Plume, 43.16
Yellow Rose, 14.66
Yellow Rose of Texas, 11.25, 11.25b
Yellow Warbler, 52.42
Yellow Wildfire, 32.26
Zinnia, 14.23
Zinnia Border, 37.96
Zinnia Bouquet, 36.51
Zodiac, 75.74

Great Titles *from* C&T PUBLISHING

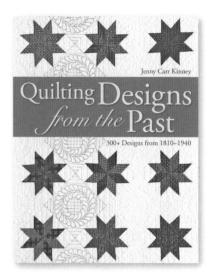

Available at your local retailer or **www.ctpub.com** *or* **800.284.1114**

For a list of other fine books from C&T Publishing,
ask for a free catalog:

C&T PUBLISHING, INC.

P.O. Box 1456
Lafayette, CA 94549
(800) 284-1114

Email: ctinfo@ctpub.com
Website: www.ctpub.com

For quilting supplies:

COTTON PATCH

1025 Brown Ave.
Lafayette, CA 94549
Store: (925) 284-1177
Mail order: (925) 283-7883

Email: CottonPa@aol.com
Website: www.quiltusa.com

C&T Publishing's professional photography services are now
available to the public. Visit us at www.ctmediaservices.com.

Note: Fabrics used in the quilts shown may not be
currently available, as fabric manufacturers keep most